Contents

NUTRITION AND BIOCHEMISTRY BSC NURSING 1 ST YEAR

PREVIOUS YEAR NURSING CHAPTER WISE SOLVED QUESTION PAPERS

RUTWIK UPENDRA BHALSHANKAR

ISBN 979-888606018-8

CHAPTER ONE

INTRODUCTION

Q 1 Nutritional problems in India .

= Nutrition

Nutrition is defined as the science of food and its relationship to health. Nutrition is food at work in the body.

Useful chemical substances derived from the food by the body are called nutrients.

Human beings require more than 45 different nutrients for their well being.

Nutrients include :

1. Carbohydrates
2. Lipids
3. Proteins Food,
4. Water
5. Minerals
6. Vitamins

Nutritional problem in india are as follow :

1. A survey in South India has revealed that about 1% children aged 1-5 years showed signs of kwashiorkor, 2% marasmus and 3-5% vitamins A dificiecy.
2. Community studies have shown that many mothers give only breast milk to children upto 2 years. Thus, no additional food is added to the child's diet.

3. Papaya which is rich in vitamin A is considered as a hot food that will cause miscarriage is avoided by pregnant women.
4. It is a belief that if a pregnant woman eats more the baby will be big and delivery difficult, so expectant mothers are not fed adequately both in quality and quantity.
5. Nutritional problems like protein energy malnutrition (PEM) and anaemia , vitamin A deficiency, this occurred in large no of children's in India
6. The diet and nutritional status of urban slum children in India is far away from satisfactory.
7. Major nutritional problem in India are protein energy malnutrition (PEM) ,vit-A deficiency, iron deficiency, anaemia and iodine deficiency disorders (IDD).

Q 2. Factors affecting food and nutrition.

= Food :

Food is vital for human existence just as air and water.

Food may be difined as anything eaten or drunk, which meets the needs of tissue building, regulation and protection of the body and its energy needs.

. **Nutrition :**

Nutrition is defined as the science of food and its relationship to health.

Nutrition is food at work in the body.

There are many factors which affect food and nutrition are as follow:

0. Biological Factors
1. Superstitions
2. Social and cultural factors
3. Religions factors
4. Income
5. Geography/availability
6. Advertising and media

7. Psychological factors

Biological Factors :

In the biological aspect two aspect which mainly influence the food and nutrition

1. Hunger : Our physiological needs provide the basic determinants of food choice. Human need energy and nutrients in order to survive.
2. Sensory aspects ; taste is consistently reported as a major influence of food behaviour.

Superstitions and Cultural Factors :

- Food habits are handed over from generation to generation in the society particularly in the developing countries.
- Though these factors have very little or no scientific basis, people rigidly adhere to them. In many parts of India pregnant women are not allowed Food, to consume papaya as it is believed that papaya produces a lot of heat in the body which in turn induces abortion. Pineapple also is not given for the same reason. .
- Consumption of a lot of garlic is for secretion of milk.
- In parts of Bengal, people believe that consumption of tongue of goat by children will make them more talkative.

Religious :

- Belief Hindus do not eat beef, since cow is an animal sacred to them.
- Among Hindus some communities do not eat fruits, onions and garlic.
- Many Hindus are vegetarians.
- Jains do not eat curds and do not eat after sunset.
- It is a custom in most communities in India that women and girls eat only after men and boys finish their eating. Thus, the health

of the female is affected as they eat poorly with the left over food.

INCOME ;

- Financial resources determine the type of food we consume.
- Depending on the availability one selects the food.
- People in lower income groups in India consume, a combination of cereals and cheaply available green leafy vegetables, roots and tubers.
- People Food of higher income groups, can choose food from all groups irrespective of season.

Geography/Availability :

- In the olden days, man would eat what ever was available to satisfy his hunger. The food he got was the type he could cultivate in his locality.
- Rice is the main food crop grown in tropical areas.
- The nutrition value of natural foods do not vary from country to country. But there is a great variation in the composition of prepared foods such as bread, biscuits, cakes etc., due to variation in recipes and basic ingredients used in different regions.

Psychological factors:

Level of stress, emotions- appetite increases during happiness but diminishes with stress

Q 3.Classification of foods.

= Food is vital for human existence just as air and water.

Food may be difined as anything eaten or drunk, which meets the needs of tissue building, regulation and protection of the body and its energy needs.

Food is the raw material from which our bodies are made.

CLASSIFICATION OF FOOD

1. Based on its origin

a. Foods of animal origin

b. Foods of vegetable origin

Based on Chemical Composition

a. Proteins

b. Fats

c. Carbohydrates

d. Minerals

e. Vitamins

Based on its Function

a. Body building foods – amino acids, proteins

b. Energy giving foods – carbohydrates (wheat, rice)

c. Protective foods – vitamins and minerals (vegetables)

Based on Nutrition Value

Five Food Group System

a. Cereals and millets

b. Pulses and legumes

c. Milk, milk products and meat

d. Fruits and vegetables

e. Fats and sugars

Based on their functions, foods are grouped into energy yielding foods, body building foods and protective foods.

- Carbohydrates, fats and proteins release energy on metabolism in our body.
- Cereals like rice, wheat, ragi and maize, roots and tubers like potato, sweet potato and tapioca are good sources of carbohydrate. Fats are more concentrated source of energy.
- Proteins are considered as body building food even though they can supply energy as well. Protein, calcium, phosphorus, iron and water are body building nutrients.
- Protein foods like milk, meat, fish, eggs, pulses, grams and nuts are essential to build our tissues and to form blood. Our body

functions are regulated by water, minerals and vitamins. They are called the protective foods. Water is necessaryfor various body processes.

- Vitamins are essential for regulating the body processes such as growth, muscular coordination of various organs and functions of several organs like eyes, ears, nose and skin.
- Minerals like Ca help in controlling blood clotting, muscular contraction and for efficiency of heart muscles. Iron is essential for blood formation. Iodine is necessary for regulating body functions through the thyroid gland.

Q 4. Function of food .

= Food is vital for human existence just as air and water.

Food may be difined as anything eaten or drunk, which meets the needs of tissue building, regulation and protection of the body and its energy needs.

Food is the raw material from which our bodies are made.

Functions of Food

1. Provide energy : Fat's are more concentrated source of energy

2. Body building : Proteins are considered as body building food even through they can supply energy as well . Protein, calcium, phosphorus, iron and water are body building nutrients.

3. Regulating the activities of the body including

a Beating of the heart

b Maintenance of body temperature

c Muscle contraction

d Clotting of blood

e Control of water balance

f Elimination of the waste products of the body

4. Provide resistance to diseases

5. Social function: Feasts are served on specific stages of life—birth, naming ceremonies, birth days, marriages etc. Prasad is distributed in temples. Pedhas are distributed to announce success in exams or birth of a baby. Laddus are associated with Deepawali and marriages, cakes with Christmas and Weddings. Refreshments served at get together and meetings create a relaxed atmostphere.

6. Psychological functions of food. Breastfeeding provides closeness and security to the child. Food also satisfy some emotional needs like security, attention and friendship and acceptance. Food can be used as a weapon to fight against diseases. An insecure child sometimes refuses food, so that mother will be concerned about the child and bow to its demand.

Q 5. Role of Food and its Medicinal Value

= **Role of Food and its Medicinal Value**

Most deficiency diseases have been eliminated in the West by abundance of food supplies. Yet diseases related to malnutrition in the form of dietary excess and imbalance are quite common in the Western countries. Four of the ten leading causes of death— heart diseases, cancer, stroke and diabetes have been linked to diet.

Poor dietary habits and a sedentary life style together account for three lakh deaths in the US every year. Dictary factors account for a third or more of all cases of both cancer and heart diseases.

A high fat diet raises risk of some types of cancer, heart diseases and obesity which in turn contribute to a number of other problems including dibetes and high blood pressure. Studies carried out have shown that the quality of diets consumed by people in the UK and USA during the period 1911–1960 have been steadily increasing and consequently the growth rate of children also was increasing during the same period. After 1960, the growth rate of children did not show any significant improvement showing that the diet had been adequate for providing maximum growth in children.

On the other hand, the rate of growth of children in the developing countries continues to be poor. The children are malnutritioned, emaciated and stunted.

CHAPTER TWO

CARBOHYDRATES

Q 1. Classification of carbohydrates

= DEFINITION OF CARBOHYDRATES

Carbohydrates may be defined as polyhydroxy aldehydes or ketones or compounds which produce them on hydrolysis

CLASSIFICATION OF CARBOHYDRATES

Carbohydrates are classified into 3 groups:

1. Monosaccharides
2. Oligosaccharides
3. Diasaccharides
3. Polysaccharides

MONOSACCHARIDES

1. Monosaccharides are the simplest group of carbohydrates and are referred to as simple sugars
2. They cannot be further hydrolysed
3. The monosaccharides are divided into different categories depending on the functional group and the number of carbon atoms
4. When the functional group in monosaccharides is an aldehyde, they are known as aldoses e.g. glyceraldehyde, glucose
5. When the functional group is a keto group, they are known as ketoses e.g. dihydroxyacetone, fructose.
6. Based on the number of carbon atoms, the monosaccharides are regarded as trioses (3C), tetroses (4C), pentoses (5C), hexoses (6C) and heptoses (7C).

OLIGOSACCHARIDES

1. Oligosaccharides contain 2 to 10 monosaccharide molecules which are liberated on hydrolysis

2. Based on the number of monosaccharide units present the oligosaccharides are further subdivided as –

a) Disaccharides (2) – e.g. Maltose

b) Trisaccharides (3) – e.g. Raffinose

c) Tetrasaccharides (4) – e.g. Stachyose

d) Pentasaccharides (5) – e.g. Fondaparinux

DISACCHARIDES

1. Disaccharides are sugars which yield two molecules of the same or different molecules of monosaccharides on hydrolysis e.g. maltose, lactose and sucrose

2 Maltose yields two molecules of glucose on hydrolysis

3. Lactose yields one molecule of glucose and one molecule of galactose on hydrolysis

4. Sucrose yields one molecule of glucose and one molecule of fructose on hydrolysis

POLYSACCHARIDES

1. Polysaccharides are sugars which yield more than ten molecules of monosaccharides on hydrolysis

2. They are of two types

a) Homo-polysaccharides – they are polymers of the same monosaccharide units e.g. – starch, glycogen, inulin, dextrin, dextran and cellulose

b) Hetero-polysaccharides - they are polymers of different monosaccharide units or their derivatives.

They are also known as mucopolysaccharides or glycosaminoglycans (GAGS)

e.g. – keratan sulfate, chondroitin sulfate, heparin and hyaluronic acid

Q 2 . Functions of carbohydrates.

= **FUNCTIONS OF CARBOHYDRATES**

1. Carbohydrates are the most abundant dietary source of energy (4 C/gm)
2. Carbohydrates are the precursors for many organic compounds such as fats and amino acids
3. Carbohydrates participate in the structure of cell membrane
4. Carbohydrates play a role in cellular functions such as cell growth, adhesion and fertilization
5. Carbohydrates serve as the storage form of energy (glycogen) to meet the immediate energy demands of the body
6. Carbohydrate derivatives are used as drugs e.g. cardiac glycosides and antibiotics
7. Lactose is the principal sugar of milk in the lactating mammary gland
8. Carbohydrates are constituents of compound lipids and conjugated proteins
9. Heparin is an anti-coagulant
10. Hetero-polysaccharides form the ground substance of tissues.

Q 3. sources of carbohydrates .

= Sources of Carbohydrates

Following are main sources of carbohydrates:

1. Starches: These are present in cereals, roots and tubers e.g., Rice,

wheat, ragi, pulses, potatoes, tapiaco, yam and colassia.

2. Sugars

a. Monosaccharides (simple sugars) glucose, fructose and galactose

b. Disaccharides (Double sugars) sucrose, lactose, maltose.
c. Polysaccharides (Complex carbohydrates) e.g., cellulose.

Q 4 .Digestion of carbohydrates :

= **DIGESTION OF CARBOHYDRATES**

DIGESTION IN MOUTH

1. Digestion of carbohydrates starts in the mouth where they come in contact with saliva during mastication

2. Saliva contains a carbohydrate splitting enzyme called salivary amylase (ptyalin)

3. Salivary amylase requires chloride ion for its activity and optimum pH of 6.7

4. It breaks down starch and glycogen into glucose and maltose

DIGESTION IN STOMACH

1. No carbohydrate splitting enzymes are present in the gastric juice

2. Some dietary sucrose may be hydrolysed to glucose and fructose by HCL

DIGESTION IN DUODENUM

1. The food reaches duodenum from the stomach, where it meets pancreatic juice

2. Pancreatic juice contains a carbohydrate splitting enzyme pancreatic amylase

3. Pancreatic amylase acts at a pH of 7.1 and requires chloride ion for its activity

4. It breaks down starch and glycogen into glucose and maltose

DIGESTION IN SMALL INTESTINE

Intestinal juice contains the following enzymes

1. Intestinal amylase

It acts at a pH of 5.5 to 6 and breaks down starch and glycogen to glucose and maltose

2. Lactase

It acts at a pH of 5.4 to 6 and breaks down lactose to glucose and galactose

3. Maltase

It acts at a pH of 5.8 to 6.2 and breaks down maltose into 2 units of glucose

4. Sucrase

It acts at a pH of 5 to 7 and breaks down sucrose into glucose and fructose

Q 5. absorption of carbohydrates.

= **ABSORPTION OF CARBOHYDRATES**

1. Carbohydrate digestion is complete when the food materials reach the small intestine and all complex carbohydrates like starch and glycogen and disaccharides are ultimately converted to monosaccharides

2. All monosaccharides are completely absorbed from the small intestine

3. No carbohydrates higher than monosaccharides can be absorbed directly into the blood and if administered intravenously are eliminated as foreign bodies

MECHANISMS OF ABSORPTION

There are 4 mechanisms for carbohydrate absorption:

1. Simple diffusion
2. Facilitated transport
3. Active transport
4. Glut2 transport

Q 6. storage of carbohydrates

1. Carbohydrates are stored in animals body in the form of glycogen.
2. Glycogen is a multibranched polysaccharide of glucose that serves as a form of energy storage in animals.
3. It is also known as animal starch
4. Glycogen primarily stored in the cells of the liver and muscles.

5. During starvation, glycogen act as primary source of energy by providing ATPs.

CHAPTER THREE

FATS

Q 1.Classification of fats / lipids .

= DEFINITION OF LIPIDS

Lipids are organic substances, relatively insoluble in water, soluble in organic solvents (alcohol, ether), related to fatty acids and utilized by living cells

CLASSIFICATION OF LIPIDS

Lipids are classified into the following groups

SIMPLE LIPIDS

These are esters of fatty acids with alcohol.

They are of two types:

a) Fats and oils (triacylglycerol)

These are esters of fatty acids with glycerol.

The difference between fat and oil is only physical.

Thus oil is a liquid while fat is a solid at room temperature

b) Waxes

These are esters of fatty acids with alcohol other than glycerol.

Cetyl alcohol is most commonly found in waxes

COMPLEX OR COMPOUND LIPIDS

These are esters of fatty acids with alcohols containing additional groups such as phosphate, nitrogenous base, carbohydrate and protein.

They are further divided as

PHOSPHOLIPIDS

These are lipids containing fatty acid, alcohol, phosphoric acid and nitrogenous base.

They are of the following types:

1. Glycero-phospholipids –

They contain glycerol as the alcohol e.g.

a) Phosphatidyl choline (lecithin)

b) Phosphatidyl ethanolamine (cephalin)

2. Sphingo-phospholipid

They contain sphingol as the alcohol. e.g.

Sphingomyelin

3. Phospho – inositide

They contain inositol as the alcohol. e.g.

Phosphatidyl inositol

GLYCOLIPIDS

These are lipids containing fatty acid, sphingol, nitrogenous base and carbohydrate e.g.

a) Cerebroside

b) Ganglioside

Q 2. Functions of lipid / fats .

= **FUNCTIONS OF LIPIDS /FAT.**

1. Lipids are constituents of membrane structure
2. Lipids regulate membrane permeability
3. Lipids are a source of fat soluble vitamins (A, D, E and K)
4. Lipids take part in regulation of cell metabolism
5. Lipids are an important source of energy (9.5 C/gm)
6. Lipids can be stored in the body in unlimited amounts
7. Lipids exert an insulating effect in the body
8. Lipids around internal organs like kidney may provide padding and protect the organ
9. Lipids are essential for proper functioning of the nervous system
10. Essential fatty acids (PUFA's) are required to be taken in the diet for normal health and growth .

Q 3. Digestion of lipids / fats .

= **DIGESTION IN THE MOUTH**

1. The enzyme lingual lipase is secreted from the dorsal surface of the tongue (Ebners gland).

2. It acts at a pH of 4 to 4.5.

3. It breaks down TG to fatty acid and glycerol

DIGESTION IN THE STOMACH

1. The enzyme gastric lipase acts at a pH of 7 to 8.

2. It requires calcium ion for its activity.

3. Activity of gastric lipase is seen when the intestinal contents are regurgitated into the stomach.

4. Fats delay the rate of emptying of the stomach and thus have high satiety value.

DIGESTION IN THE SMALL INTESTINE

1. Pancreatic juice enters the small intestine through the pancreatic duct and bile enters the small intestine through the bile duct.

2. Secretion of pancreatic juice is stimulated by the hormones secretin and Cholecystokinin – Pancreozymin (CCK-PZ)

3. Bile salts help in emulsification of fats (breakdown of fats into smaller units).

4. Pancreatic lipase acts at a pH of 6 and breaks down triglycerides into fatty acids and glycerol.

5. The enzyme cholesterol esterase breaks down cholesterol esters and phospholipase breaks down phospholipids.

Q 4 . Absorption of fats

ABSORPTION OF LIPIDS

1. The resynthesized triglycerides in the intestinal epithelial cells cannot pass to lymphatics or to the portal blood as they are insoluble in water.

2. Triglycerides get covered with a layer of phospholipid, cholesterol and apoprotein to from the lipoprotein chylomicron.

3. Chylomicrons are soluble; they pass out through the intestinal epithelial cell and enter the blood and lymphatics.

Q 5. Sources of fat .

= Important Sources of Fats

RICH SOURCES FAT %

Pure oils and fats 100

Ghee and vanaspathi 100

Butter 80–81

Good sources:

Nuts and oil seeds 40–60

Milk powder 26

Eggs 14

Meat and fish 10–15

Fair sources:

Cow's milk 4

Buffalo milk 7

Whole pulses 3.5

Whole cereals and millets 2.3

Q 6. Describe the effect of deficiency and excess of fat in diet .

= **Excess of Fat :**

Our body need healthy fat for energy and other functions .

But too much fat can cause cholesterol to bulid up in our arteries (blood vessels .)

Saturated fat Raise your LDL (bad) cholesterol increase your risk for the heart disease and stroke.

Cholesterol deposition in blood vessels is major problem of excessive fat in diet.

Obesity : Taking in more calories than you can expend in an average day make you gain weight.

Constipation : Diet that are high in fat can affect your digestive organs. If a diet is high in saturated fat to the determinant of your fibre intake , you may become constipated frequently.

Cancer : An excessive of fat and shortage fibers in your diet can cause cancerous cellular growth .

Deficiency of fat :

Not getting enough fat (or carbs or protein) means your body isn't getting enough calories .

People who eat less fat tends to eat more carbs and more carbs with less fat is a combination that can leave you felling hungry. A lot . The reason for this your blood sugar wont be stable.

Some effects of fat deficiency on Humans are as follows :

1. Skin problems : When essential fatty acids are missing from our diet it can cause skin problems . A essential fatty acid deficiency increases loss of water from your skin which result in dry, scaly, rash.
2. Vision problems : EPA and DHA are important components of the retina. DHA helps from the pigment rhodopsin , which you need for your brain to into the image you see .

CHAPTER FOUR

PROTEINS

Q 1.Classification of proteins .

= **DEFINITION**

Proteins are polymers of amino acids.

They are the fundamental structural components of the body

CLASSIFICATION OF PROTEINS

Proteins can be classified in four ways

1. Classification based on shape and size
2. Functional classification
3. Classification based on chemical nature and solubility
4. Nutritional classification

CLASSIFICATION ON THE BASIS OF SHAPE AND SIZE

On the basis of shape and size proteins are classified into 2 types – fibrous and globular

FIBROUS PROTEINS

When the axial ratio of length to width of a protein molecule is more than 10, it is called a fibrous protein eg – keratin and collagen

GLOBULAR PROTEINS

When the axial ratio of length to width of a protein molecule is less than 10, it is called globular protein eg – haemoglobin and ribonuclease

FUNCTIONAL CLASSIFICATION OF PROTEINS

Based on the functions they perform, proteins are classified as

1. Structural proteins – they are involved in formation of structures of the body e.g. - keratin of hair and nail and collagen of bone

2. Enzyme proteins – all enzymes are protein in nature e.g. – hexokinase, pepsin

3. Transport proteins – proteins involved in transport of substances e.g. –

a) Haemoglobin transports oxygen

b) Albumin transports bilirubin

4. Hormonal proteins- some of the hormones are protein in nature e.g. Insulin and growth hormone

5. Contractile proteins – proteins which take part in muscle contraction. e.g. – Actin and myosin

6. Storage proteins – proteins involved in storage of substances

e.g. – Ferritin stores iron

7. Genetic proteins – proteins involved in genetic function e.g. – Nucleoprotein

8. Defence proteins – proteins involved in defence function e.g. – Immunoglobulins

9. Receptor proteins – protein which act as receptors e.g. – Cytokine receptor, integrin

10. Respiratory proteins – proteins involved in the function of respiration e.g. – Haemoglobin and cytochrome

CLASSIFICATION BASED ON CHEMICAL NATURE AND SOLUBILITY

According to this proteins are classified into 3 groups – simple, conjugated and derived

SIMPLE PROTEINS

These are proteins which on complete hydrolysis yield only amino acids.

e.g.

1. Protamine – they are small molecules rich in arginine
2. Histones – they are found in association with DNA
3. Albumin – normal serum level is 3.5 to 5 gm %
4. Globulin – normal serum level is 1.8 to 3.6 gm %

5. Gliadin – it is rich in proline

6. Glutelin – it is rich in glutamic acid

7. Scleroproteins – these proteins have great stability and very low solubility and form supporting structures in the body e.g. –

a) Keratin of hair

a) Collagen of bone

b) Elastin of connective tissue

CONJUGATED PROTEINS

1. Conjugated proteins are simple proteins combined with a non protein group called prosthetic group

2. Protein part is called apoprotein and the entire molecule is called holoprotein

3. E.g. nucleoprotein, mucoprotein, glycoprotein, chromoprotein, phosphoprotein, lipoprotein and metalloprotein

NUTRITIONAL CLASSIFICATION OF PROTEINS

From the nutritional point of view proteins are classified as

1. Complete proteins

2. Partially incomplete proteins

3. Incomplete proteins

COMPLETE PROTEINS

These proteins have all the essential amino acids in the required proportions by the human body to promote good growth e.g. egg albumin and milk casein

PARTIALLY INCOMPLETE PROTEIN

These proteins are partially lacking one or more essential amino acids and hence can promote moderate growth e.g. – wheat and rice proteins (lack lysine and threonine)

INCOMPLETE PROTEINS

These proteins completely lack one or more essential amino acids, hence do not promote growth at all e.g. – gelatin (lacks tryptophan), maize/corn (lacks tryptophan and lysine)

Q2. Functions of proteins.

= FUNCTIONS OF PROTEINS

1. Primary Tissue Building

Protein is the fundamental structural material of every cell in the body. The primary functions are to repair the worn out, wasted or damaged tissue and build up new tissue. Thus, protein meets the growth needs and maintains tissue health during adult years. In addition to body building functions, protein has other body functions related to energy, water balance, metabolism and body's defence mechanism.

1. **Energy System**

Carbohydrates are the primary fuel source for the body assisted by fat as stored fuel. In times of need (e.g., Starvation) protein may also furnish additional fuel to sustain heat and energy. Fuel supplied by protein is 4 k cal/gm (like carbohydrates).

1. **Water Balance**

Plasma proteins, especially albrumin helps to control water balance throughout the body by exerting osmotic pressure to maintain internal circulation of body fluids and capillary blood flow.

3. **Metabolism**

Protein aids metabolic functions through enzymes, hormones and

transport agents. Digestive and cell hormones are hormones that control metabolic functions. Enzymes are necessary for the digestion of Carbohydrates (amylase) fats (lipase) and proteins (proteases) are all proteins. Proteins also act as vehicles in which nutrients are carried throughout the body. Lipoproteins are necessary to transport fats in the water soluble blood supply. Other examples are haemoglobin and transferrin, the iron transport proteins in blood. Hormones such as insulin and glucagen are also proteins that have a major role in the metabolism of glucose.

4. **The Body Defence System**

Protein is used to build special white blood cells (lymphocytes) and antibodies as part of body's immune system to help defend against infection and diseases.

5. **Energy Supply**

A small part of body's need for energy (about 6 to 12%) is supplied

by products of protein metabolism.

Q 3. Kwashiorkor.

= Kwashiorkor is due to inadequate protein in the diet despite an adequate calories intake

Children are more affected by kwashiorkor than adult . it typically than adults. It typically starts after the child has breast milk has been replaced by diet with low in protein, although it can occur in infants if the mother is protein deprive .

Kwashiorkor is a form of severe protein malnutrition characterized by edema and an enlarged liver with fatty infiltrates.

It cause by sufficient calories intake but with insufficient protein consumption, which distinguishes it from marasmus.

Kwashiorkor is occurred in area of famine or poor food supply.

Kwashiorkor is a severe form of malnutrition associated with a deficiency in dietary protein , the extreme lack of protein causes osmotic imbalance in gastro-intesteinal system causing swelling of the gut diagnosis as an edema or retention of water.

Sign and symptoms :

The defining sign of kwashiorkor in a malnourished child is pitting edema. (Swelling of ankles and feet) .

Other signs includes a distended abdomen, an enlarged liver wuth fatty infiltrate , thinning of liver ,loss of teeth , skin depigmentation and dermatitis.

Generally the disease can be treated by adding protein to the diet, however, it can have a long term impact on a child physical and mental development, and in severe cases may leads death.

Q 4 .Importance of protein in children .

= Children need adequate amount of protein for good health .

Proteins are essential for the development of both the brain and the body, and maintenance of structure such as bone, muscle and skin.

As a child hood is a phase of growth and development. The protein requirement of children are significantly higher than that of adults. So it is ensure that their children grt enough protein every day .

Protei is an importent component of every cell in the body . Children body need more proteins because they are at growing stage, Proteins also make enzymes, hormones, and other body chemicals. Protein is an important building block of bones, muscles, cartilages, skin and blood.

Protein is quickly digested providing a rapid rise in amino acids that may helps increases muscle mass and strength. It may also reduce appetite and promote fat loss.

If protein deficiency occurs in children during growth period produces kwashiorkor and marasmus.

Protein calorie malnutrition is one of the largest nutritional problem of India.

Q6. Malnutrition.

= **Definition of malnutrition** : faulty nutrition due to inadequate or unbalanced intake of nutrients or their impaired assimilation or utilization .

Malnutrition occurs when the body doesn't get enough nutrients.

Causes include a poor diet , digestive conditions or another disease .

Malnutrition is a condition that occurs that result from eating a diet in which one more nutrients are not enough or are to much that the diet causes health problems.

It may involve calories , protein, carbohydrates, fat , vitamins, or minerals.

No enough nutrient is called under nutrition or undernourishment while too much is called overnutrition.

Malnutrition is often used to specifically refer to undernoutrishment where an individual is not getting enough calories, proteins, or micronutrients.

If undernutrition occurs during pregnancy,or beforetwo years of age it may results in a permant problems with a physical and mental development.

Extreme undernourishment knows as starvation may have symptoms that include a short height, thin body, very poor energy levels , and swollen legs and abdomen.

People also often get infectious and are frequently cold . The symptom of micronutrients deficiencies depend on the micronutrient deficiencies depend on the micronutrient that is lacking.

Undernourishment is most often due to not enough high quality food being available to eat . this is food being available to eat This is often related to high food price and poverty.

There are two main ypes of undernutition :

1. Protein energy malnutrition (PEM)
2. Dietary deficiencies .

1 . Protein energy malnutrition has two severe forms : (a) Marasmus (A lack of protein and calories) (b) Kwashiorkor (A lack of protein)

2 . Dietary deficiencies : A lack of iron , iodine , vitamins, and minerals.

We can beat malnutrition by giving food security to people . Gov to be take a proper actions and efferts to bring modern agricultural techniques to increase food quality and quantity and increases nutrients contains.

Q 7. Clinical features of marasmus and kwashiorkor.

=

Marasmus

Weight loss

Dehydration , Dirrhea.

Stomach shrinkage

Severe wasting of muscles

· Loss of subcutaneous fat (Limbs appear as skin and bones)

· Skin is dry and atrophic

· Anaemia

· Eye lesions due to Vitamin A deficiency

· Irritability and fretfulness

· Diarrhoea

· Dehydration

· Body temperature is sub-normal

· Failure to thrive

· Wrinkled skin - Old man's face

· Grossly underweight

kwashiorkor

Inability to grow or gain weight ,

Edema ,or swelling of the hands and feet.

Stomach bulging

Growth failure

· Oedema of the face and lower limbs

· Muscle wasting

· Fatty liver

· Anorexia(loss of appetite)

· Diarrhoea

· Change in the colour, sparse, soft and thin hair.

· Change in the colour of the skin(hypo and hyperpigmentation)

· Anaemia

· Vitamin A deficiency

· Angular stomatitis(Cracks in the corners of mouth)

· Cheilosis (inflammation and cracks in lips)

· Moon face

Q 8. Difference between kwashiorkor and marasmus .

=

Table 10.5: Differences between Kwashiorkor and Marasmus	
Kwashiorkor	**Marasmus**
It develops in children whose diets are deficient of protein.	It is due to deficiency of proteins and calories.
It occurs in children between 6 months and 3 years of age.	It is common in infants under 1 year of age.
Subcutaneous fat is preserved.	Subcutaneous fat is not preserved
Oedema is present.	Oedema is absent.
Enlarged fatty liver.	No fatty liver.
Ribs are not very prominent.	Ribs become very prominent.
Lethargic	Alert and irritable.
Muscle wasting mild or absent.	Severe muscle wasting
Poor appetite.	Voracious feeder.
The person suffering from kwashiorkor needs adequate amounts of proteins.	The person suffering from marasmus needs adequate amount of proteins, fats and carbohydrates.

Difference between kwashiorkor and marasmus

Q 9. Protein energy malnutrition .

= *Protein Energy Malnutrition*

Protein Energy Malnutrition (PEM) is defined as a range of pathological conditions arising from coincident lack of varying proportions of protein and calorie, occurring most frequently in infants and young children and often associated with infection (WHO,1973) PEM affects children under 5 years of age belonging to the poor underprivileged communities.

Under nutrition is a complex condition with multiple deficiencies such as proteins,energy and micro nutrient deficiencies often occurring together. According to WHO, malnutrition is an underlying factor in over 50 % of the 10 – 11 million yearly deaths of children under 5 years.

Classification of PEM

Protein energy malnutrition may be classified into three types as follows:

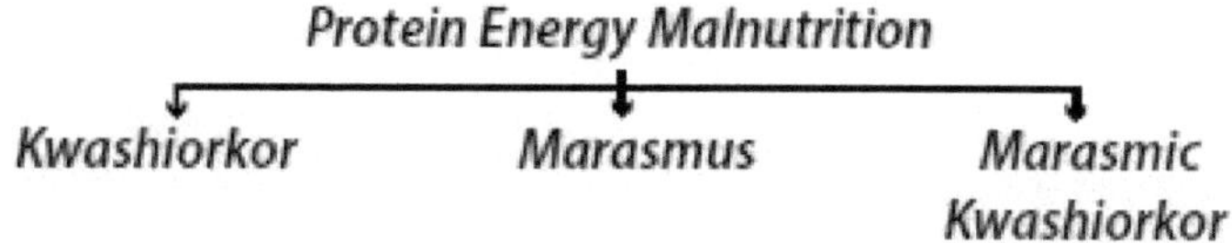

Fig 10.6: Classification of PEM

I. Kwashiorkor

Kwashiorkor is due to inadequate protein in the diet despite an adequate calories intake

Children are more affected by kwashiorkor than adult . it typically than adults. It typically starts after the child has breast milk has been replaced by diet with low in protein, although it can occur in infants if the mother is protein deprive .

Kwashiorkor is a form of severe protein malnutrition characterized by edema and an enlarged liver with fatty infiltrates.

It cause by sufficient calories intake but with insufficient protein consumption, which distinguishes it from marasmus.

Clinical signs and symptoms

Growth failure

· Oedema of the face and lower limbs

· Muscle wasting

· Fatty liver

· Anorexia(loss of appetite)

· Diarrhoea

· Change in the colour, sparse, soft and thin hair.

· Change in the colour of the skin(hypo and hyperpigmentation)

· Anaemia

· Vitamin A deficiency

· Angular stomatitis(Cracks in the corners of mouth)

· Cheilosis (inflammation and cracks in lips)

· Moon face

ii. Marasmus

This is caused by severe deficiency of proteins and calories in the diet. The important features are as follows:

Severe wasting of muscles

· Loss of subcutaneous fat (Limbs appear as skin and bones)

· Skin is dry and atrophic

· Anaemia

· Eye lesions due to Vitamin A deficiency

· Irritability and fretfulness

· Diarrhoea

· Dehydration

· Body temperature is sub-normal

· Failure to thrive

· Wrinkled skin - Old man's face

· Grossly underweight

III. Marasmic Kwashiorkor

Children suffering from this disease show signs of both kwashiorkor and marasmus.

CHAPTER FIVE

ENERGY

Q 1. Define BMR. Explain factors affecting basal metabolic rate .

= **Definition of BMR**

BMR is defined as the energy expenditure of a subject at complete

physical and mental rest, awake (and not during sleep) having normal body temperature and in the post absorption state (12 hours after the last meal) and 8–12 hours after any significant physical activity.

Factors Affecting BMR

BMR differs among different individuals. It depends on:

a. Variable factors

b. Invariable factors

Variable Factors Affecting BMR

a. Nutritional state: BMR is low in starvation and undernourishment as compared to well fed state. Starvation leads to

an adaptive decrease in BMR, which results from a decrease in lean body mass.

b. Body size or surface area: The BMR is directly proportional to the

surface area of the subject. Larger the surface area, greater will be the heat loss and equally higher will be the heat production and BMR.

c. Body composition: The BMR is proportionate to lean body mass

(LBM). LBM is the body weight minus non-essential (storage

Food, Nutrition and Health 303

triacyl glycerol) weight. Adipose tissue is not as metabolically active as lean body mass. BMR is often expressed as per kilogram of lean body mass or fat free mass. Therefore, higher the percentage of adipose tissue in the body lower the BMR/ kg body weight.

d. Endocrinal or hormonal state: In hyperthyroidism, the BMR is

increased and in hypotheproidism it may be decreased by upto 40%, leading to weight loss.

e. Environmental temperature or climate: In colder climate the BMR

is higher and in tropical climate the BMR is proportionately low. Stress, anxiety and disease states, especially infections, fever, burns and cancer also increases the BMR.

f. Drugs: Smoking (nicotine), coffee (coffine) and tea (theophylline)

increase the BMR whereas β-blockers tend to decrease energy expenditure.

Invariable Factors Affecting BMR

a. Gender or sex: The BMR of males is slightly higher than that of

females particularly due to:

i. Womens lower percentage of muscle mass (lean body mass) and higher percentage of adipose tissue (that has lower rate of metabolism) when compared to men of the same body weight, and

ii. The difference in sex hormone profile of the two genders.

b. Age: Decrease in BMR with increasing age is probably related to loss of muscle mass (lean body mass) and replacement of muscle with adipose tissue that has lower rate of metabolism.

Q 2. Body mass index .

= BODY MASS INDEX : QUETELETS INDEX

The basal mass index is used as a reference standard for assessing

the prevalence of obesity in the community.

BMI = Weight in kg /Height in meters

Ideal body mass index for Indian woman = 19–24

Ideal body mass index for Indian man = 20–26

Once the BMI exceeds the normal limit, the person can be termed as overweight or obese.

CHAPTER SIX

VITAMINS

Q 1.Classification of vitamins :

= Vitamins may be regarded as organic compounds required in the diet in small amounts to perform specific biological functions for normal maintenance of optimum growth and health of the organism.

Although vitamins have little chemical similarities their metabolic functions have been described as

1. Membrane stabilizers
2. Hydrogen and electro donor & acceptor
3. Hormones & coenzymes.

Classification of vitamins

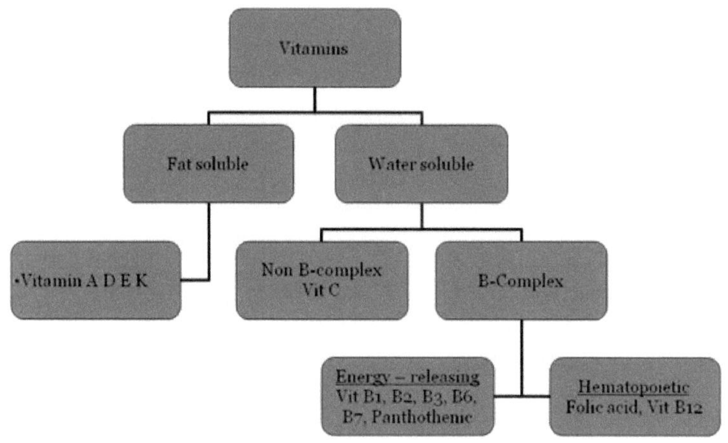

Classification of vitamins

Fat-soluble vitamins

a. Vitamin A, D,E and K are know as fat or lipid – soluble vitamins.
n. Their availability in the diet, absorption and transport are associated with fat.
n. They are soluble in fats and oils and also the fat solvents (alcohol, acetone etc.)
n. They are stored in the liver and adipose tissue.
n. They are not readily excreted in urine. But with feceas via the enterohepatic circulation
n. Excess consumption may lead to accumulation and toxic effects.

Water soluble vitamins

n. Heterogeneous group of compounds since they differ chemically from each other.
n. Common character – solubility in water.
n. Readily excreted in urine and not toxic to body.

n. Not stored in large quantities in the body (except vitamin B12).
n. Stores depleted within weeks and deficiency symptoms results.
n. Hence need to be continuously supplied through the diet.

Q 2. Functions of vitamin A

n. = Fat soluble vitamin A (retinoids), refers to 3 preformed compounds

1. Alcohol – retinol
2. Aldehyde – retinal / retinaldehyde
3. Acid – retinoic acid

n. Vitamin A is required for a variety of functions such as

1. Vision
2. Proper growth and differentiation
3. Reproduction
4. Maintenance of epithelial cells.
5. Vitamin A is required for normal reproduction
6. Vitamin A is required for epithelialization and is essential to maintain healthy epithelial tissue
7. Vitamin A is required for the construction of normal bone and teeth
8. Vitamin A is required for glycoprotein synthesis
9. Vitamin A is required for the synthesis of chondroitin sulfate
10. Vitamin A plays a role in cell differentiation and cell division
11. Vitamin A is involved in protein synthesis
12. Vitamin A plays a role in DNA metabolism
13. Carotenes function as antioxidants and reduce the risk of cancers initiated by free radicals

Q 3 . deficiency manifestations of vitamin

= **VITAMIN A DEFICIENCY**

1. Retinol deficiency depresses the re-synthesis of rhodopsin and interferes with the function of rods resulting in night blindness
2. In Vitamin A deficiency sperm cells do not mature and in females there may be abortion
3. In Vitamin A deficiency the skin becomes dry, scaly and rough. These changes are called keratinization
4. There is dryness of the conjunctiva and cornea, which is known as xerophthalmia
5. White opaque spots, known as Bitots spots appear on the conjunctiva
6. Cornea becomes keratinized, opaque, soft and ulcerated. This is known as keratomalacia
7. Keratinization occurs in the mucous membrane of the respiratory tract leading to increased susceptibility to infection and lowered resistance to disease
8. Vitamin A deficiency causes arrested bone development
9. The teeth become unhealthy with chalky deposits on the surface

Q 4. Write the sources of vitamin A .

= **DIETARY SOURCES**

1. Animal sources – liver, kidney, egg yolk, milk, cheese, butter and cod liver oil
2. Vegetable sources – carotenes – carrots, spinach, pumpkins, mango and papaya

n. Foods provide vitamin A either in the preformed state (directly as retinol or retinyl esters of fatty acids) from animal sources such as milk, butter, egg and fish.

n. Or its precursor carotenoids, especially carotene, derived from leafy vegetables and yellow- and orange-coloured fruits and vegetables.

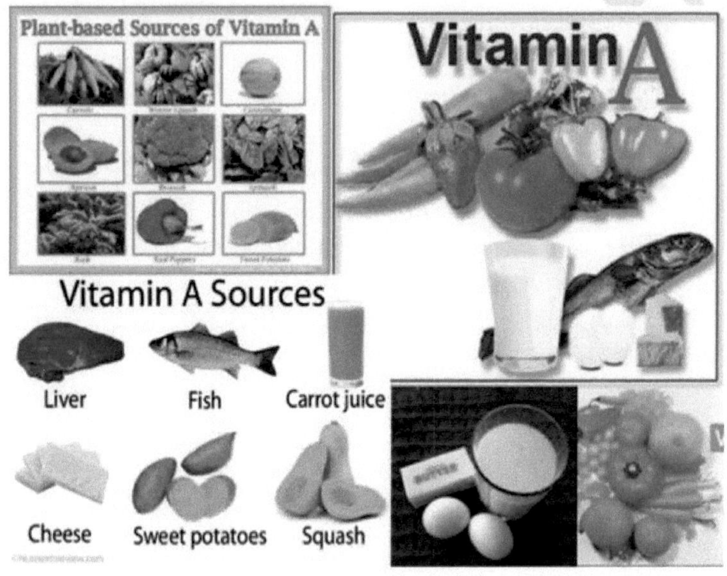

Sources of vitamin A

Q 5. Functions of vitamin C .

= **FUNCTIONS**

1. Vit C is required as a coenzyme in hydroxylation of proline and lysine

Hydroxyproline and hydroxylysine are important constituents of collagen

Thus vitamin C is required for collagen synthesis

2. Vit C is required for bone formation

3. Vit C enhances iron absorption by keeping it in the reduced ferrous

4. Vit C is essential for the hydroxylation of tryptophan to hydroxy tryptophan in the synthesis of serotonin

5. Vit C is required for the oxidation of P hydroxy phenyl pyruvate to homogentisic acid in tyrosine metabolism

6. Vit C is required for the reduction of dihydrofolate (FH_2) to tetrahydrofolate (FH_4).

Tetrahydrofolate (FH_4) is the active form of folic acid

7. Vit C is required for the synthesis of steroid hormones

8. Vit C is a strong antioxidant.

It spares vitamin A and vitamin E from oxidation

9. Vit C enhances the synthesis of immunoglobulins

10. Vit C increases the phagocytic activity of leucocytes

11. Vit C is required for the formation of mucopolysaccharides

12. Vit C is required for the functional activity of osteoblasts and fibroblasts

13. Vit C is required for the formation of ferritin

14. Vit C is required for the electron transport chain

15. Vit C activates the enzyme arginase and inhibits the enzymes urease and amylase

16. Vit C is required as a coenzyme for the conversion of dopamine to norepinephrine

17. Vit C is required for the formation of carnitine

18. Vit C is required for the alpha oxidation of fatty acids

19. Vit C plays a role in reduction of blood cholesterol level

20. Vit C plays an important role in the reaction of the body to stress

Q 6. Deficiency of vitamin C.

= DEFICIENCY OF VITAMIN C

1. Vitamin C deficiency causes a disease called scurvy.

2. The capillaries are fragile and there is a tendency to haemorrhage.

3. The haemorrhage may be subcutaneous, subperiosteal or internal.

4. Wound healing is deficient due to decreased formation of collagen.

5. Poor teeth formation.

6. Gums are swollen, spongy and bleed on slightest pressure.

7. In severe infection there may be secondary infection, loosening and falling of teeth.

8. Mineralization of the bone is poor and the bones are weak and easily fractured.

9. Bones and joints are extremely painful.

10. Hypochromic microcytic anemia.

11. Elderly bachelors and widowers, who prepare their own food, are particularly prone to the development of vitamin C deficiency.

This is called bachelor scurvy.

Q 7. Functions of vitamin D.

= Calcitriol increases the intestinal absorption of calcium and phosphorus by increasing the synthesis of calcium binding protein. This protein increases calcium absorption by the intestine

2. In the osteoblasts of the bone, calcitriol stimulates calcium uptake for deposition as calcium phosphate. Thus calcitriol is essential for bone formation

3. Calcitriol increases the reabsorption of calcium and phosphorus by the kidney and thus decreases their excretion in the urine .

Q 8 . Deficiency manifestations of vitamin D .

= **DEFICIENCY OF VITAMIN D**

There are 3 types of vitamin D deficiency:

1. Rickets

2. Osteomalacia

3. Renal osteodystrophy

RICKETS

1. Vitamin D deficiency in children is known as rickets

2. In the absence of vitamin D the osteoblast proliferation is not accompanied by vascularization and mineralization at the normal rate

3. The bones become soft

4. Bending of long bones gives rise to deformities such as bow legs and knock knees

5. The ankles, knees, wrists and elbows are swollen

6. The fontanelles do not close properly giving rise to hot cross bun appearance of the head

7. The ribs give a beaded appearance, known as ricket rosary

8. The chest gives a pigeon breast appearance

9. Teeth erupt late and are deformed

OSTEOMALACIA

1. Vitamin D deficiency in adults is known as osteomalacia

2. Osteomalacia is seen in pregnancy and lactation, when there is additional requirement of vitamin D and drainage of it in the milk

3. Osteomalacia is also seen in women who observe purdah and in areas where sunshine is scanty

4. In osteomalacia the bones become soft and are easily fractured

5. It particularly affects the pelvic bones

RENAL OSTEODYSTROPHY

1. It is also known as renal rickets

2. It is seen in patients with chronic renal failure

3. Renal rickets is mainly due to decreased synthesis of calcitriol by the kidney

4. It can be treated by the administration of calcitriol

Q 8. List sources of thiamine (B_1) and effect of its deficiency .

= **DIETARY SOURCES**

1. Plant sources – rice, wheat, peas, beans and nuts
2. Animal sources – liver, meat, eggs, pork and milk

DEFICIENCY FEATURES

1. The deficiency of thiamine results in a condition called beriberi (Sinhalese – I cannot, said twice)

2. Cardiovascular features – these include palpitation, dyspnoea, cardiac hypertrophy, which may progress to congestive cardiac failure

3. Neurological features

a) There is ascending, symmetrical, peripheral polyneuritis

b) Numbness in the legs

c) Pins and needles sensation in the legs

d) Mental depression and irritability

e) In some cases there may be acute hemorrhagic encephalitis, which is known as Wernicke's encephalopathy

4. GIT features

These include decreased gastric motility, nausea, weakness, fever and vomiting.

5. Metabolic features

a) There is accumulation of pentose sugars in the RBCs due to retardation of transketolation reaction

b) There is accumulation of pyruvate in the tissues and blood due to decreased activity of pyruvate dehydrogenase

6. Types of beriberi

It is of two types

a) Wet beriberi – in this oedema is present due to congestive cardiac failure and low plasma albumin level

b) Dry beriberi – oedema is absent.

CHAPTER SEVEN

MINERALS

Q 1. Classification of minerals .

= The mineral elements constitute only a small proportion of the body weight and there is a wide variation in their body content

Minerals perform several vital functions which are absolutely essential for the existence of man

These functions include calcification of bone, blood clotting, neuromuscular irritability, acid base balance and water-electrolyte balance.

CLASSIFICATION

The elements of the body are divided into 5 major groups

GROUP 1

1. These are components of macromolecules such as carbohydrates, proteins and lipids.

2. Examples

a) Carbon (C)

b) Hydrogen (H)

c) Oxygen (O)

d) Nitrogen (N)

GROUP 2

1. These are nutritionally important minerals or principal elements

2. Their daily requirement is more than 100 mg

3. Their deficiency can prove fatal

4. They are also known as macro elements

5. Examples

Sodium (Na)

Potassium (K)

Chloride (Cl)

Calcium (Ca)

Phosphorus (P)

Magnesium (Mg)

Sulfur (S)

GROUP 3

1. These are known as trace elements

2. They are essential elements and their requirement is less than 100 mg

3. Their deficiency can lead to serious disorders

4. Examples

a) Chromium (Cr)

b) Cobalt (Co)

c) Copper (Cu)

d) Iodine (I)

e) Iron (Fe)

f) Manganese (Mn)

g) Molybdenum (Mb)

h) Selenium (Se)

i) Zinc (Zn)

GROUP 4

1. These are additional trace elements

2. They may be possibly essential

3. Their exact role is not known

4. Examples

Cadmium (Cd)

Nickel (Ni)

Silicon (Si)

Tin (Sn)

Vanadium (Vn)

GROUP 5

1. These are not essential elements and may be toxic
2. They have no known function in the body
3. They may enter the body through polluted air, water, soil or food
4. Examples
Arsenic (As)
Cyanide (Cn)
Mercury (Hg)

Q 2. Functions of minerals

= **Functions**

Intracellular calcium is involved in:
a. Muscle contraction.
b. Release of hormones, neurotrausmitter and neuromodulators.
c. Activation of a number of enzymes.
d. Glycogen metabolism.
e. Cell division.
Extracellular calcium provide calcium ion for the:
a. Maintenance of intracellular calcium.
b. Bone mineralisation.
c. Blood coagulation.
d. Membrane excitability.
e. Plasma membrane potential.

Q 3. Factors affecting iron absorption

= **FACTORS WHICH DECREASE IRON ABSORPTION**

1. Phytates present in corn, soya and cereals decrease iron absorption
2. Oxalates, present in leafy vegetables and chocolates decrease iron absorption
3. A diet with high phosphorus content decreases iron absorption
4. Tea, coffee and eggs decrease iron absorption

5. Dietary fibers decrease iron absorption
6. Alkaline pH decreases iron absorption
7. Impaired absorption of iron is found in malabsorption syndromes such as steatorrheoa
8. In patients with partial or total surgical removal of stomach / intestine, iron absorption is impaired
9. Parasitic infection (hookworm) decreases iron absorption

Q 4. Write sources and effect of deficiency of iron.

= DIETARY SOURCES

1. Rich sources – organ meats (liver, heart and kidneys)
2. Good sources – leafy vegetables, pulses, cereals, fish, dried fruits, apple and meat
3. Poor sources – milk, wheat and rice
4. Haeme iron which comes from animal products and is from haemoglobin and myoglobin is efficiently absorbed (20 to 30 %)
5. Non haeme iron which is present in plants is inefficiently absorbed (1 to 5 %)

CLINICAL FEATURES OF IRON DEFICIENCY

1. Hypochromic microcytic anemia
2. Blood Hb below 12gm %
3. Apathy – dull and inactive
4. Sluggish metabolic activities
5. Retarded growth
6. Loss of appetite
7. Serum ferritin decreased
8. Serum transferrin decreased
9. RBC protoporphyrin increased

Q 5. FUNCTIONS OF CALCIUM

= **FUNCTIONS OF CALCIUM**

1. Calcium is required for bone formation
2. Calcium plays a role in muscle contraction
Calcium increases the interaction between actin and myosin
3. Calcium is necessary for transmission of nerve impulse
4. Calcium influences cell membrane structure
5. Calcium plays a role in the transport of water and ions across the cell membrane
6. Calcium activates the enzymes pancreatic lipase, ATPase and succinate dehydrogenase
7. Calmodulin is a calcium binding regulatory protein Calcium calmodulin complex activates the enzymes adenylate cyclase and protein kinase
8. Certain hormones exert their action through the mediation of calcium and thus calcium acts as a second messenger or third messenger for such hormonal action e.g. – epinephrine and anti diuretic hormone
9. Calcium is required for the release of certain hormones from the endocrine glands e.g. insulin, parathyroid hormone and calcitonin

Q 6. Write the factors interfering in absorption of calcium .

= **FACTORS WHICH INTERFERING IN CALCIUM ABSORPTION**

1. Phytates present in cereals form insoluble calcium salts and inhibit calcium absorption
2. Oxalates present in vegetables like cabbage and spinach form insoluble calcium salts and inhibit calcium absorption
3. High content of dietary phosphorus results in the formation of insoluble calcium phosphate and inhibits calcium absorption
4. Free fatty acids inhibit calcium absorption by reacting with calcium to form insoluble calcium soap . This is particularly

observed when fat absorption is impaired

5. High pH (alkaline conditions) inhibits calcium absorption

6. High content of dietary fibers interferes with calcium absorption

7. High content of magnesium in the diet decreases calcium absorption

8. High content of iron in the diet inhibits calcium absorption .

CHAPTER EIGHT

WATER AND ELECTROLYTES

Q 1. Regulation of water metabolism .

= Water is the commonest liquid with the most uncommon properties. Water content of the body changes with age. It is almost 75% in the newborn and decreases to less than 50% in older individuals. Water content is maximum in brain tissue and least in adipose tissue.

Regulation of Water Metabolism

• Antidiuretic hormone or Vasopressin which has got the property to enhance water reabsorption

2. Hypothalamus known as a thirst centre. Besides this, osmoconcentration of plasma also stimulates supraoptic and paraventricular nuclei

3. Adrenal Cortex. Aldosterone has controll excretion of sodium and potassium by the kidneys

4. Rennin-Angiotensin system. Angiotensin II stimulates the synthesis and secretion of aldosterone and the release of vasopressin, and thereby increases renal absorption of Na+ and H2O.

5. Prostaglandins. They may also increase urinary loss of water by inhibiting the antidiuretic effect of vasopressin and by increasing the urinary sodium.

6. Solutes. Osmotic effect of Na+ helps to retain water in extracellular fluids. Elevation in plasma Na+ raises the ECF volume in primary aldosteronism while an increase in urinary Na+ raises the urinary water output in Addisons disease. K+ helps to retain water in the cells, whereas, plasma proteins do help to retain water in the body by their osmotic effects. Increase in urinary urea or excretion of glucose in urine increases osmotically the urinary loss of water (osmotic diuresis).

Q 2.Composition of body fluids .

= Total water in the body is about 40 L. It is distributed into two major compartments:

1. Intracellular fluid (ICF): Its volume is 22 L and it forms 55% of the total body water.

2. Extracellular fluid (ECF): Its volume is 18 L and it forms 45% of the total body water.

ECF is divided into 5 subunits:

i. Interstitial fluid and lymph (20%)
ii. Plasma (7.5%)
iii. Fluid in bones (7.5%)
iv. Fluid in dense connective tissues like cartilage (7.5%)
v. Transcellular fluid (2.5%) that includes:
a. Cerebrospinal fluid
b. Intraocular fluid
c. Digestive juices
d. Serous fluid – intrapleural fluid, pericardial fluid and peritoneal fluid
e. Synovial fluid in joints
f. Fluid in urinary tract.

Volume of interstitial fluid is about 12 L. Volume of plasma is about 2.75 L. Volume of other subunits of ECF is about 3.25 L. Water moves between different Compartments.

Q 3. Functions and requirement of water

= Importance (Functions) of Water

1. It acts as a carrier of nutritive elements to tissues and removes waste materials from tissues.

2. It provides the media in which chemical reactions of the body take place.

3. The fluidity of blood is because of water.

4. It is the solvent for electrolytes and regulates the electrolytic balance of the body. It maintains the equilibrium of osmotic pressure extended by the solutes dissolved in water.

5. It is a regulator of body temperature, because of its high specific heat, it can absorb or give off heat without any appreciable change in temperature. Also, because of its high latent heat, it provides the mechanism for the regulation of heat loss by sensible (sweating) and insensible (through the respiratory tract) perspiration.

Q 4. Over hydration .

= **Definition**

Overhydration, also called water excess or water intoxication, is a condition in which the body contains too much water.

Description

Overhydration occurs when the body takes in more water than it excretes and its normal sodium level is diluted. This can result in digestive problems, behavioral changes, brain damage, seizures, or coma.

Overhydration is an imbalance of fluids. It happens when your body takes in or holds on to more fluid than your kidneys can remove.

Drinking too much water or not having a way to remove it can cause water levels to build up. This dilutes important substances in your blood. Endurance athletes, such as those who run marathons and triathlons, sometimes drink too much water before and during an event.

Overhydration is an imbalance of fluids. It happens when your body takes in or holds on to more fluid than your kidneys can remove.

Drinking too much water or not having a way to remove it can cause water levels to build up. This dilutes important substances in your blood. Endurance athletes, such as those who run marathons and triathlons, sometimes drink too much water before and during an event.

treatement for overhydration depends on how severe your symptoms are and what caused the condition.

Treatments may include:

- cutting back on your fluid intake
- taking diuretics to increase the amount of urine you produce
- treating the condition that caused the overhydration
- stopping any medications causing the problem
- replacing sodium in severe cases

Q 5. Dehydration

= In physiology, dehydration is a deficit of total body water,[1] with an accompanying disruption of metabolic processes. It occurs when free water loss exceeds free water intake, usually due to exercise, disease, or high environmental temperature. Mild dehydration can also be caused by immersion diuresis, which may increase risk of decompression sickness in divers.

Signs and symptoms

The hallmarks of dehydration include thirst and neurological changes such as headaches, general discomfort, loss of appetite, decreased urine volume (unless polyuria is the cause of dehydration), confusion, unexplained tiredness, purple fingernails and seizures.

Cause

Risk factors for dehydration include but are not limited to: exerting oneself in hot and humid weather, habitation at high altitudes, endurance athletics, elderly adults, infants, children and people living with chronic illnesses.

Dehydration can also come as a side effect from many different types of drugs and medications.

Treatment : Management of dehydration

The treatment for minor dehydration that is often considered the most effective is drinking water and stopping fluid loss. Plain water restores only the volume of the blood plasma, inhibiting the thirst mechanism before solute levels can be replenished . Solid foods can contribute to fluid loss from vomiting and diarrhea. Urine concentration and frequency will customarily return to normal as dehydration resolves .

CHAPTER NINE

COOKERY RULES & PRESERVATION OF NUTRIENTS

Q 1. Food preservation .

= Food preservation is the science dealing with the process of dealing with the prevention of decay or spoilage of food, thus allowing it to be stored in a fit condition for future use. The process used may be varied with the period of storage. It may be as simple as boiling milk to preserve it for 24 hours or pickling vegetables, fish or meat to last for a year.

Need for Food Preservation

There is always a shortage of food in developing countries like India due to demands of the growing population. Increasing production to meet the shortage results in wastage due to inadequate facilities available for storage and preservation. It is therefore all the more important to improve and expand facilities for storage and preservation of food. Preservation increases availability of foods, thus improving the nutrition of the people. Availability of seasonal foods throughout the year also helps in stabilising prices of food stuffs.

PRINCIPLES OF FOOD PRESERVATION

1. Prevention or delay of microbial decomposition by

a. Keeping out micro-organisms (asepsis).

b. Removal of micro-organism, e.g. by filtration.

c. Inhibiting the growth and activity of microbes by the use of lower temperature, drying, anaerobic conditions or chemicals.

2. Destroying the microorganisms by radiation or by heat.

3. Preventing or delay of self decomposition of the food by

a. Destroying or inactivation of food enzymes e.g., by blanching or boiling.

b. Prevention or delay of purely chemical reactions e.g. prevention of oxidation by antioxidants.

c. Prevention of damage by insects and rodents.

Q 2. METHODS OF FOOD PRESERVATION

= METHODS OF FOOD PRESERVATION

1. Bacteriostatic Methods

Which inhibit the growth and multiplication of micro-organisms in food e.g., Freezing, dehydration, pickling, salting and smoking.

2. Bactericidal Methods

In which the microorganisms are killed, e.g., cooking, canning and irradiation.

a. Cold Storage and Freezing

Refrigeration is widely used both in homes and in commercial plants as a means of maintaining the low temperature necessary for storage of perishable foods. Micro-organisms are much less active at low temperature even though they may not be destroyed by severe cold. Fresh milk, and fish are kept just above the freezing point.

A refrigerator thermometer is kept in the refrigerator at all times. Left over foods from a meal should not stay out of refrigeration longer than two hours. Certain fruits and vegetables **also keep better when cold.**

b. Boiling

Boiling food at 100°C kills all vegetative cells and spores of moulds and yeast but not bacterial spores. Cooking of rice, vegetables, meat etc. is usually done in homes by boiling. Many foods are preserved at home by boiling e.g., Milk. Cooked food can be preserved from 12 to 24 hours at room temperature.

c. Canning

If the effectiveness of pasteurization and sterilization has to last for a long time, the material thus treated must be protected from fresh contamination by canning. Various foods eg. Fruit juices,milk, baby foods, soups and fish are preserved by canning. The food is first sterilized at temperature above 100°C for a few seconds and then cooked and filled in presterilised containers in a sterile atmosphere. There is some loss of heat labile vitamins during the process of canning.

d. Addition of Salt or Sugar

Certain chemicals are useful in preserving food, either by retarding or preventing the growth of microorganisms. There may be either added to the product or produced in it by fermentation. Dry salting is used for the preservation of tamarind, raw mango, amla, fish and meat. Pickling of mango, lemon, fish and meat is by addition of 15 to 20% salt. Rosagulla and gulabjamoon are preserved by sugar syrup. The principle is high osmotic pressure produced by salt or sugar.

e. Jams and Marmalades

Jams and marmalades are prepared by boiling the fruit pulp or shredded fruit peels with sugar (above 55% by weight) to a thick consistency, firm enough to hold the fruit tissues in position. Later on, they are packed hot into glass jars or tin cans and sealed. The same process is used for jellies except that fruit juices are used in place of fruit pulps. The high concentration ofsugar (68%) binds the moisture making it not available for microorganism to grow and multiply. Anaerobic conditions are obtained by sealing. Application of heat kills most of the moulds and yeast. All these increase the shell life of the products.

f. pH

Low pH inhibits the growth of many organisms. Vinegar used in pickling is acetric acid. Citric acid is added to many fruit squashes, jams and jellies to increase acidity and to prevent mould growth. Formation of curd from milk is an example of lactic acid produced from lactose. The lactic acid inhibits the growth of bacteria. By adding certain condiments along with salt, certain foods like mangoes, vegetables, meat and fish are preserved.

g. Chemical Preservation

Benzoic acid is used to preserve fruits, fruit juices, squash and jams because it is soluble in water and easily mixes up with food products. Potassium metabisulphite or sodium metabisulphite is used to preserve colourless food stuff such as fruits, juices and squash. These preservatives, on reaction with fruit acids liberate SO2 (sulphur dioxide) which is quite effective in killing the harmful microbes present in food. SO2 is a bleaching agent and cannot be used as a preservative for coloured food materials.

Q 3.Prevention of food adulteration act, 1954 .

= Prevention of Food Adulteration Act 1954 (PFA) The prevention of food adulteration act 1954 came into effect from june 1, 1955. The purpose of the Act is to ensure that food articles sold to the consumers are pure and wholesome, also to prevent deception or fraud and to ensure fair trade practices. The act was amended in 1964 and 1976 to plug the loopholes and to ensure deterant punishment to the offenders. As per the Act, food can be considered adulterated when any one of the following modes (or acts) are resorted to:

i. Admixture of inferior or cheaper substance.

ii. Extraction of certain quality ingredients from the food.

iii. Preparing or packing under insanitary conditions.

iv. Sale of insect infected food.

v. Obtaining the food from a diseased animal.

vi. Incorporation of a poisonous component.

vii. Entry of injurious constituents from the container used.

viii. Use of colouring matter other than or in greater quantities than that approved for the food.

ix. Sale of substandard products which may or may not be injurious to health. These are all prohibited acts under the prevention of Food adulteration act. Persons found guilty of selling such adulterated food, can be convicted. The severity of sentence would depend on the gravity of the offence.

Q 4. Food fortification .

= Food fortification or enrichment is the process of adding micronutrients (essential trace elements and vitamins) to food. It can be carried out by food manufacturers, or by governments as a public health policy which aims to reduce the number of people with dietary deficiencies within a population. The predominant diet within a region can lack particular nutrients due to the local soil or from inherent deficiencies within the staple foods; addition of micronutrients to staples and condiments can prevent large-scale deficiency diseases in these cases.

As defined by the World Health Organization (WHO) and the Food and Agricultural Organization of the United Nations (FAO), fortification refers to "the practice of deliberately increasing the content of an essential micronutrient, ie. vitamins and minerals (including trace elements) in a food, so as to improve the nutritional quality of the food supply and to provide a public health benefit with minimal risk to health", whereas enrichment is defined as "synonymous with fortification and refers to the addition of micronutrients to a food which are lost during processing".

Examples of fortification in foods.

Many foods and beverages worldwide have been fortified, whether a voluntary action by the product developers or by law.

The Food Fortification Initiative lists all countries in the world that conduct fortification programs, and within each country, what nutrients are added to which foods, and whether those programs are voluntary or mandatory. Vitamin fortification programs exist in one or more countries for folate, niacin, riboflavin, thiamin, vitamin A, vitamin B6, vitamin B12, vitamin D and vitamin E. Mineral fortification programs include calcium, fluoride, iodine, iron, selenium and zinc.

Q 6. Food additives .

= Food additives are substances added to food to preserve flavor or enhance its taste, appearance, or other qualities. Some additives have been used for centuries; for example, preserving food by pickling (with vinegar), salting, as with bacon, preserving sweets or using sulfur dioxide as with wines. With the advent of processed foods in the second half of the twentieth century, many more additives have been introduced, of both natural and artificial origin. Food additives also include substances that may be introduced to food indirectly (called "indirect additives") in the manufacturing process, through packaging, or during storage or transport.

Categories .

Food additives can be divided into several groups, although there is some overlap because some additives exert more than one effect. For example, salt is both a preservative as well as a flavor.

Food coloring.

Colorings are added to food to replace colors lost during preparation or to make food look more attractive.

Fortifying agents.

Vitamins, minerals, and dietary supplements to increase the nutritional value

Color retention agents.

In contrast to colorings, color retention agents are used to preserve a food's existing color.

Emulsifiers.

Emulsifiers allow water and oils to remain mixed together in an emulsion, as in mayonnaise, ice cream, and homogenized milk.

Flavors .

Flavors are additives that give food a particular taste or smell, and may be derived from natural ingredients or created artificially.

Flavor enhancers .

Flavor enhancers enhance a food's existing flavors. A popular example is monosodium glutamate. Some flavor enhancers have their own flavors that are independent of the food.

Q 7. Methods of cooking .

= Cooking Media Food can be cooked in various media or no media at all. Air, water, steam and fat or their combinations are used as cooking media. Food can be cooked by a combination of media e.g., Upma and halwa involve the combination of fat and water. Cooking in Air Grilling, roasting and baking take place in air. Roasting and baking are essentially the same. The term roasting is used to meat cooking and baking is used for breads, buns, cakes and biscuits. Food is cooked partially in dry heat and partially in moist heat. Cooking in Water Boiling or simmering involves cooking in water. The medium transferring heat is water.

1. Roasting.

a. Split roasting: Is done only with good quality meats. The food is brought in contact with direct flame in front of a bright fire. The food is pasted over with fat and is turned regularly to ensure even cooking and browning. Roast meats have an excellent flavour and are served in large hotels and special restaurants

e.g., Barbe eued meat.

b. Oven roasting:

This is done in a closed oven with the aid of fat. First class meat, poulty and vegetables are put into a fairly hot oven for 5 to 10 minutes and temperature is lowered to allow the joint to be cooked. Cooking in a moderate oven for a longer time produces a better cooked joint than cooking at a higher temperature for shorter period. Aluminium foil is used. The joint is larded or raised with fat. This cooking is an improvement on oven roasting as the meat retains its moisture and flavour.

c. Pot roasting: This is for cooking small joint and boils when no oven is available. A thick heavy pan is available and enough fatis melted to cover the bottom of the pan. The joint is browned when the fat is hot. The joint is then placed on a couple of skewers to prevent the joint from sticking to the pan. The pan is then covered tightly with the lid and cooked over a very low fire.

2. Baking

Bread, cakes, pastries, puddings, potatoes and vegetables are cooked by baking. The food is surrounded by hot air in a closed oven. The action of the dry heat is modified by steam arising the food being cooked.

3. Frying

Here the food is brought in contact with hot fat. Even though fried foods are a bit difficult to digest, if the frying is carefully carried out, the fried food is suitable for normal people. Frying provides variety, keeping quality is better and the food is really apetising.

4. Boiling

Food is cooked by surrounding it by boiling or simmering liquid (stock or water). Only sufficient amount of liquid should be used just to cover the items to be cooked. Vegetables grown above the ground are cooked in boiled salted water and vegetables grown below the ground are cooked in cold salted water. Dry vegetables are cooked in cold water. Salt is added only after the vegetables become soft. Fish is put into hot liquid and allowed to simmer.

5. Poaching

Poaching is cooking slowly in a minimum amount of liquid which is not allowed to boil but kept below boiling point. Fish, eggs and fruits are poached. When poaching eggs, a little vinegar is added to the liquid for quick coagulation and to prevent disintegration.

9. Microwave Cooking

Microwave is electromagnetic radiation similar to that found in radio, radar or TV. Microwaves penetrate the food and are absorbed. The heating is very fast. Foods placed in the microwave oven are heated by microwaves from all the directions. This helps in easy cooking.

10. Pressure Cooking

Steam cooking are of three types—Steam cooking, waterless cooking and pressure cooking. In steaming, food is cooked by steam from added water. In waterless cooking the steam originates from food itself. Pressure cooking is a device to reduce the cooking time by increasing the pressure so that the boiling point is quickly reached. The food is cooked as a result of steam condensation on food e.g., rice, dal, puttu.

Q 8. Principals of Weaning .

=Weaning is the process of gradually introducing an infant human or another mammal to what will be its adult diet while withdrawing the supply of its mother's milk.

The process takes place only in mammals, as only mammals produce milk. The infant is considered to be fully weaned once it is no longer fed any breast milk.

Basic principles

The basic principles of baby-led weaning are:

- At the start of the process the baby is allowed to reject food, and it may be offered again at a later date.
- The child is allowed to decide how much it wants to eat. No "fill-ups" are to be offered at the end of the meal with a spoon.
- The meals should not be hurried.
- Sips of water are offered with meals.
- Initially, soft fruits and vegetables are given. Harder foods are lightly cooked to make them soft enough to chew on even with bare gums.
- Food given is free of added salt and sugar.
- Food is not cut into bite-sized pieces until the baby has mastered object permanence and the pincer grasp.
- Initially, food is offered in baton-shaped pieces or in natural shapes that have a 'handle' (such as broccoli florets), so that the baby can get a good grip and the food is visible for babies that have not yet mastered object permanence.
- Foods with clear danger, such as peanuts, are not offered.

- Foods can be offered to the baby on a spoon, but the baby is allowed to grab the spoon and the adult helps the baby guide it to the mouth.

CHAPTER TEN

BALANCED DIET

Q 1.Balanced diet

= *Introduction*

A diet is all that we consume in a day. And a balanced diet is a diet that contains an adequate quantity of the nutrients that we require in a day. A balanced diet includes six main nutrients, i.e. Fats, Protein, Carbohydrates, Fibre, Vitamins, and Minerals.

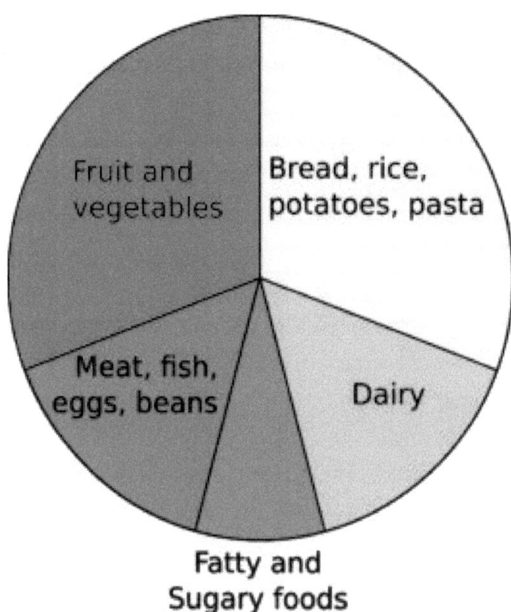

All these nutrients are present in the foods that we eat. Different food items have different proportions of nutrients present in them. The requirements of the nutrients depend on the age, gender, and health of a person.

Importance of a Balanced Diet

The following are the importance of a balanced diet :

- Balanced Diet leads to a good physical and a good mental health.
- It helps in proper growth of the body.
- Also, it increases the capacity to work
- Balanced diet increases the ability to fight or resist diseases.

Components of a balanced diet

Some components of a balanced diet are as follows :

Fats

Some part of our energy requirement is fulfilled by fats. Fats can be found in fatty foods such as butter, ghee, oil, cheese, etc.

Proteins

We need proteins for growth purposes and to repair the wear and tear of the body. Protein also helps in building muscle. It is found in dairy products, sprouts, meat, eggs, chicken, etc

Carbohydrates

We need the energy to process and it is fulfilled by carbohydrates. Carbs provide us energy. Carbohydrates can be found in rice, wheat, chapati, bread, etc. Cereals are our staple food.

Minerals and Vitamins

Vitamins, Minerals, and Fibre improve the body's resistance to disease. We mainly obtain it from vegetables and fruits. Deficiency diseases like Anemia, Goitre, etc can be caused due to lack of mineral in the body.

Q 2. PLANNING BALANCED DIETS

= **Balanced diet**

A balanced diet is one which contains different types of foods such as cereals, pulses and vegetables in such quantities and proportion that the nutritional requirements are adequately met and a small provision is made for extra nutrients to withstand short duration of leanness.

1. A balanced diet should provide 60-70 percent of calories from carbohydrate, 10-20 percent from protein and 20-25 percent from fat.

2. Calorie allowance can be $\pm$ 50, while for all other nutrients minimum RDA must be met.

3. Energy from cereals should not be more than 75 percent.

4. Include two cereals in one meal eg:- rice and wheat.

5. To improve protein quality the ratio of cereal protein to pulse protein should be 4:1.

6. Two to three serving of pulses should be taken a day.

7. Include atleast one medium size fruit. The fruit can be given raw without much cooking.

8. Five servings of fruits and vegetables should be included in a day

9. The diet should include minimum 100ml milk per day.

10. Foods rich in fibre should be included.

11. One third of the nutritional requirements, at least calorie and protein should be met by lunch or dinner.

Q 3. recommended dietary allowances

= **Recommended Dietary Allowance:** The RDA, the estimated amount of a nutrient (or calories) per day considered necessary for the maintenance of good health by the Food and Nutrition Board of the National Research Council/ National Academy of Sciences.

Q 4. Therapeutic diet for a patient with hypertension

= **Reduce sodium (salt)** — Reducing the amount of sodium you consume can lower blood pressure if you have high or borderline-high blood pressure.

The main source of sodium in the diet is the salt

Reduce alcohol — Drinking an excessive amount of alcohol increases your risk of developing high blood pressure.

Eat more fruits and vegetables — Adding more fruits and vegetables to your diet may reduce high blood pressure or protect against developing high blood pressure. A strict vegetarian diet may not be necessary.

Eat more fiber — Eating an increased amount of fiber may decrease blood pressure. The recommended amount of dietary fiber is 20 to 35 grams of fiber per day. Many breakfast cereals are excellent sources of dietary fiber. More information about increasing fiber is available separately. (See "Patient education: High-fiber diet (Beyond the Basics)".)

Eat more fish — Eating more fish may help to lower blood pressure, especially when combined with weight loss [3].

Caffeine — Caffeine may cause a small rise in blood pressure, although this effect is usually temporary. Drinking a moderate amount of caffeine (less than 2 cups of coffee per day) does not increase the risk of high blood pressure in most people.

One of the steps your doctor may recommend to lower your high blood pressure is to start using the **DASH diet.**

DASH stands for Dietary Approaches to Stop Hypertension. The diet is simple:

Eat more fruits, vegetables, and low-fat dairy foods

Cut back on foods that are high in saturated fat, cholesterol, and trans fats

Eat more whole-grain foods, fish, poultry, and nuts

Limit sodium, sweets, sugary drinks, and red meats .

Q . 6. Plan a balanced diet for female adolescent .

== The Adolescent (12-16 years)

This is an age of rapid growth and intense activity. Individual variation is marked in this age group. A number of physical, emotional and mental changes occur in this period of life. Girls mature between 11 and 13 years.

The transition phase from childhood to adulthood is known as adolescence with speeded physical, biochemical and emotional development. It is during this period that the final growth occurs.

There are many changes in the body due to hormones.

Girls must

give special attention to foods rich in protein, iron and other nutrients

necessary for synthesis and regeneration of red blood cells. Girl’s diet

should include iron rich foods such as dahls, leafy green vegetables,

dried fruits, egg, liver and red meat (if acceptable).

Fruits and vegetables every day. Your teen should eat 2 cups of fruit and 2 ½ cups of vegetables every day (for a 2,000 calorie diet).

1,300 milligrams (mg) of calcium daily. Your teen should eat three 1-cup servings of low-fat or fat-free calcium-rich foods every day. Good sources include yogurt or milk. One-cup equivalents include 1½ ounces of low-fat cheddar cheese or 2 ounces of fat-free American cheese.

Protein to build muscles and organs. Your teen should eat 5½ ounces of protein-rich foods every day. Good sources include lean meat, poultry, or fish. One-ounce equivalents of other protein sources include ½ cup of beans or tofu, one egg, a tablespoon of peanut butter, and ½ ounce of nuts or seeds.

Whole grains for energy. Teens should get 6 ounces of grains every day. One-ounce equivalents include one slice of whole grain bread, ½ cup of whole grain pasta or brown rice, 1 cup of bulgur, or 1 cup of whole grain breakfast cereal.

Iron-rich foods. Boys double their lean body mass between the ages of 10 and 17, needing iron to support their growth. Girls need iron for growth too, and to replace blood they lose through menstruation. Good sources of iron include lean beef, iron-fortified cereals and breads, dried beans and peas, or spinach.

Limiting fat. Teens should limit their fat intake to 25 to 35 percent of their total calories every day and they should choose unsaturated fats over saturated fats whenever possible. Healthier, unsaturated fats include olive, canola, safflower, sunflower, corn, and soybean oils; fatty, coldwater fish like salmon, trout, tuna, and whitefish; and nuts and seeds.

Q 7. write the features of diet and sample menu for school children .

= School-age children (ages 6 to 12) need healthy foods and nutritious snacks. They have a steady but slow rate of growth and usually eat 4 to 5 times a day (with snacks). Many food habits, likes, and dislikes are set during this time. Family, friends, and the media (chiefly TV) effect their food choices and eating habits. School-age children are often willing to eat a wider variety of foods than their younger siblings. Eating healthy after-school snacks is important, too, as these snacks may contribute up to one-fourth of the total calorie intake for the day.

Calories and Proteins

The requirements of calories are increased steadily in this age group.

It increases further during adolescence. The increased requirements

of proteins would meet demands of growth. Girls require more protein

to meet the needs of approaching menarche.

Minerals

10-12 years old children require more calcium than adults to meet

skeletal growth. As the blood volume increases, there is an increased

demand for iron.

Sample diet for school children .

Always serve breakfast, even if it has to be "on the run." Some ideas for a quick, healthy breakfast include:

Fruit

Milk

Bagel

Cheese toast

Cereal

Peanut butter sandwich

Take advantage of big appetites after school by serving healthy snacks, such as:

Fruit

Vegetables and dip

Yogurt

Turkey or chicken sandwich

Cheese and crackers

Milk and cereal

Q . 8. Soft diet .

= SOFT DIET

This bridges the gap between acute illness and convalescence. It is used in acute infection following surgery and for patients unable to chew. The soft diet is

a. Made of simple foods

b. Easily digestable

c. Contains no fibre

d. Near to a normal diet

e. Not highly spiced or seasoned.

Soft Diet It bridges the gap between acute illness and convalescence. It may be used in acute infections, following surgery, and for patients who are unable to chew. The soft diet is made up of simple, easily digestable food and contains no harsh fibre. Patients with dental problems are given mechanically soft diet. It is often modified further for certain pathologic conditions as bland and low residue diets. In this diet, three meals with intermediate feedings should be given.

Foods to eat on a soft foods diet

- canned fish and canned poultry
- fruit juice and vegetable juice
- white rice
- egg noodles
- white bread
- mashed potatoes
- bananas
- mangoes
- avocados

Q 9. Fluid diet .

= The fluid diet is divided into two types as below:

a. Clear fluid diets

b. Full fluid diets.

CLEAR FLUID DIETS

Clear fluids are prescribed for patients with marked intolerance. An acute illness may produce nausea, vomiting, anorexia, distention and diarrhoea. Clear fluid diets are meant to provide very few calories and make up the water loss in the body. Clear fluid diets include:

a. Tender coconut water

b. Clear fruit juices

c. Glucose water

d. Albumin water

e. Clear vegetable or meat soup

f. Whey water

The clear fluids are used for 1 or 2 days till the patient is able to retain and digest a more liberal liquid diet.

FULL FLUID DIET

This diet bridges the gap between clear fluid and soft diet. These consist of inclusion of eggs, milk, cereal, porridges, conjees or gruels, vegetable, chicken or mutton soup, fruit milk shakes etc. This diet will meet the minimum requirement of all protein calories, vitamins and minerals.

It is used following operations in acute gastritis, acute infections and in diarrhoea.

CHAPTER ELEVEN

ROLE OF NURSE IN NUTRITIONAL

Q 1. Mid-day meal programme .

= Midday Meal Programme (MDMP)

MDMP is also called the school lunch programme with following principles:

a. The meal should be a supplement and not a subsititute to the home diet.

b. The meal should supply at least one-third of the total energy requirement and half of the protein used.

c. Cost of the meal should be reasonably low.

d. Cooking should be easy, no complicated cooking process should be involved.

e. As far as possible, locally available foods should be used to reduce its cost.

f. The menu should be frequently rotated to avoid monotony.

A model menu for a mid-day school meal

Food stuffs gms per day/child

Cereals and millets 75gms

Pulses 30 gms

Oil and fats 8 gms

Leafy vegetables 30 gms

Non-leafy vegetables 30 gms

Mid-Day Meal Scheme aims to :

1. Avoid the pressurizing hunger children face in the classrooms
2. Some students don't come to school because they don't have a suitable meal. This will increase the enrollment as well
3. The attendance levels in many government schools have been seen dropping since past years. This will, therefore, help the school's maintain a good attendance and also increase literacy.
4. It improves socialization among castes
5. Malnutrition is a big problem and people are still not aware of it. This step provides awareness towards malnutrition and also initiates a healthy meal to avoid it.
6. Mid-day meal scheme needs a lot of labour and cooking. So it will provide employment to a lot of women.

Q 2. Integrated child development scheme

= Launched in 1975, Integrated Child Development Scheme (ICDS) is a unique early

childhood development programme, aimed at addressing malnutrition, health and also

development needs of young children, pregnant and nursing mothers.

ICDS consists of 4 different components, namely:

1. Early Childhood Care Education & Development (ECCED)

2. Care & Nutrition Counselling

3. Health Services

4. Community Mobilisation Awareness, Advocacy &Information, Education andCommunication.

Integrated Child Development Services (ICDS) is a government programme in India which provides food, preschool education, primary healthcare, immunization, health check-up and referral services to children under 6 years of age and their mothers.

The following services are sponsored under ICDS to help achieve its objectives:

1. Immunization
2. Supplementary nutrition
3. Health checkup
4. Referral services
5. Pre-school education(Non-Formal)
6. Nutrition and Health information

Q 3. Vitamin A deficiency programme .

= . Vitamin A Prophylaxis Programme

As a part of the National Programme of Prevention of Nutritional blindness is to administer a single massive dose of an oily preparation of vitamin A containing 200,000 IU (110 mg of retinol palmitate) orally to all preschool children of 1-5 years of age in the community every 6 months through peripheral health workers. The scheme developed based on the technology by National Institute of Nutrition, Hyderabad and launched by the ministry of Health and Family Welfare in 1970 is a remarkable success in preventing blindness.

Q 4. National iodine deficiency disorder programme .

= Control of Iodine Deficiency Disorders

The National Goitre Control Programme was launched by the government of India in 1962, in the conventional goitre belt in the Himalayan region to supply iodinised salt in place of common salt. But surveys slowed that the deficiency disorder was more widespread with nearly 145 million people with iodine deficiency.

As a result, a major national programme—the IDD control programme was initiated in 1986 with the objective to replace the entire edible common salt with iodinised salt.

Q 5.Role of nurse in nutritional programmes .

= Nurses are concerned about the nutritional status of all their patients. What people eat affects their health from conception through old age. Chronic malnutrition affects physical and mental development. In industrialized societies. Many diet related diseases result from nutritional excess than undernourishment.

For example, Coronary heart disease is the result of excessive intake of saturated fats and cholesterol, cancer is linked to high fat, fibre and alcohol consumption, hypertension, a risk factor for strokes is associated with intake of excessive calories and salt; liver diseases are associated with heavy alcohol consumption and diabetes mellitus with excessive calorie intake and subsequent obesity.

Community health nurses are often the contact between community residents and health care system. Because of frequent and extended contact with patients in the community, nurses have excellent opportunities to provide information and counselling about the importance of nutrition in preventing illness and promoting health

ROLE OF COMMUNITY HEALTH NURSE IN NUTRITION

1. The community health nurse will have to study the food habits

of people in her community, their views etc.

2. She must impart the knowledge of the importance of good nutrition without hurting their cultural habits.

Role of Nurse in Nutritional Programmes 391

3. She must use all media of health education in nutrition education.

4. She needs to demonstrate simple receipes which are affordable

and locally available.

5. She will identify the malnutritioned children and refer them to appropriate nutrition programmes.
6. She assists in nutrition rehabilitation programmes.
7. She also takes part in nutrition research.

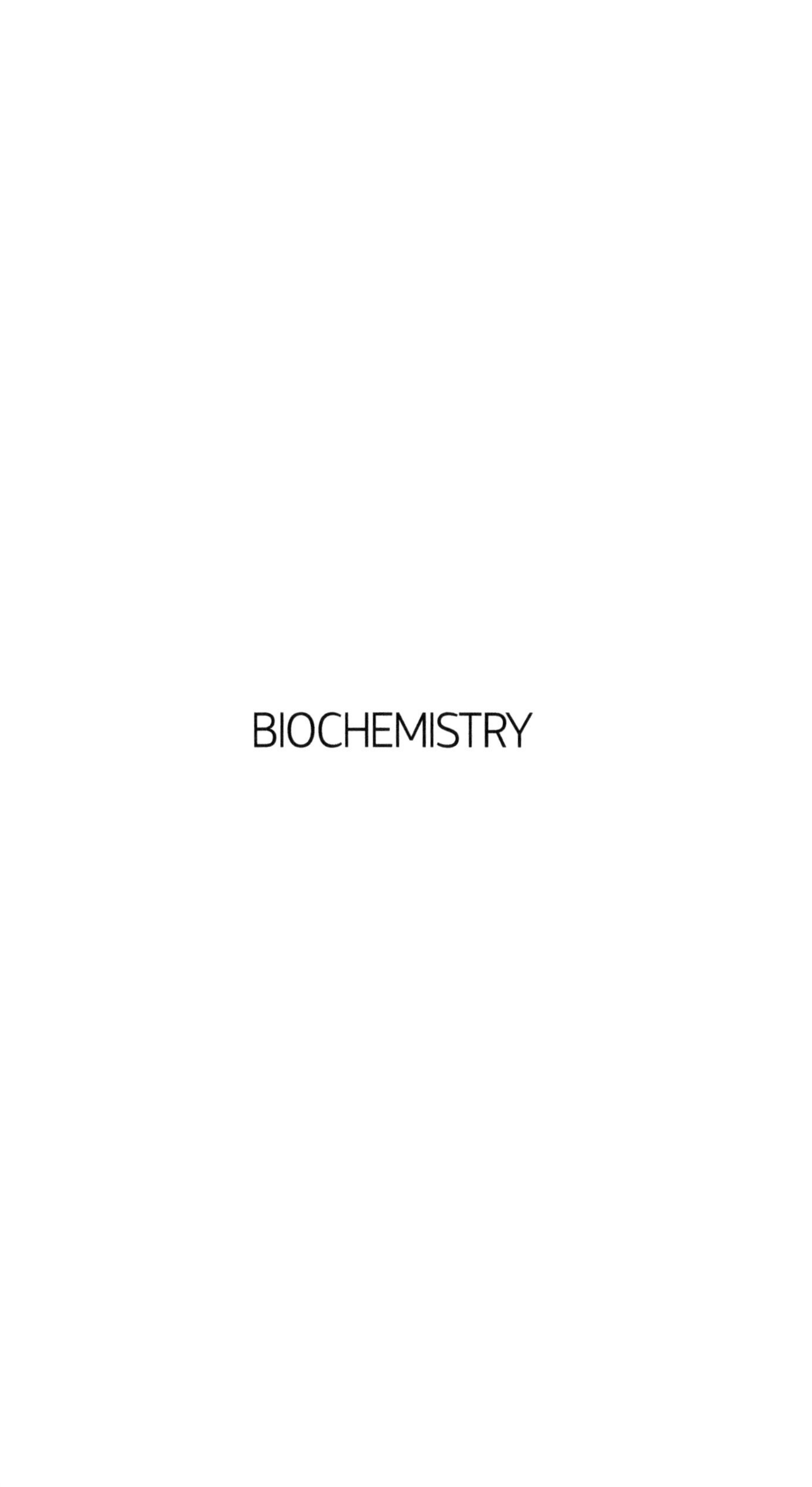

BIOCHEMISTRY

CHAPTER TWELVE

INTRODUCTION

Q 1. Structure and function of mitochondria.

= **Structure :**

1. Mitochondria are rod like or filamentous bodies, with dimensions of 1 * 3 microns
2. About 2000 mitochondria, occupying one fifth of the total cell volume are present in a typical cell.
3. The mitochondrion consists of 5 distinct parts

    a. The outer membrane
    b. The inner membrane
    c. The inter-membrane space
    d. The cristae
    e. The matrix

4. The mitochondria are composed of a double membrane system
5. The outer membrane is smooth and completely envelops the organelle
6. The inner membrane is impermeable to ions and small molecules

7. The inner membrane is highly folded to form cristae, which greatly increase its surface area .
8. The interior ground substance is called the mitochondrial matrix
9. The mitochondrial matrix contains a circular double stranded DNA (mtDNA), RNA and ribosomes .

Functions :

1. The mitochondria are the centers for metabolic oxidative reactions and are regarded as the power house of the cell.
2. Mitochondria are the centers for cellular respiration and energy metabolism
3. The ETC and ATP synthesizing system are located on the inner mitochondrial membrane
4. The inner surface of the inner mitochondrial membrane has specialized particles (that look like lollipops), the phosphorylating subunits, which are the centers for ATP production
5. The matrix also participates in the synthesis of haeme and urea
6. Mitochondria are the principal producers of ATP in the aerobic cells
7. ATP, the energy currency, generated in the mitochondria, is exported to all parts of the cell to provide energy for cellular work.

Q 2. Difference between prokaryote and eukaryote cell .

=

DIFFERENCES BETWEEN PROKARYOTIC CELL AND EUKARYOTIC CELL			
CHARACTERISTIC			
	PROKARYOTIC	CELL	EUKARYOTIC CELL
1.	**Size**	Small (1 to 10 microns)	Large (10 to 100 microns)
2.	**Cell membrane**	Cell is enveloped by	Cell is enveloped by
		rigid cell wall	flexible plasma membrane
3.	**Sub-cellular**	Absent	Present
Organelles			
4.	**Nucleus** Nucleus well defined	Not well defined	
		DNA is found as nucleoid. Histones absent	Surrounded by membrane DNA associated with histone
5.	**Energy**	Mitochondria	
	Metabolism	absent. Enzymes of	
		energy metabolism	Enzymes of energy
		bound to membrane	metabolism located
6.	**Cell division**	Fission	in mitochondria
7.	**Cytoplasm**	Organelles and	
		cytoskeleton	Mitosis
		absent	Organelles and cytoskeleton present.

CHAPTER THIRTEEN

STRUCTURE AND FUNCTION OF CELL MEMBRANE

Q 1. Describe the fluid mosaic structure of cell membrane .

= **STRUCTURE OF CELL MEMBRANE / FLUID MOSAIC MODEL OF CELL MEMBRANE**

1. The fluid mosaic model proposed by Singer and Nicholson (1972) is the most acceptable model for membrane structure

2. The membranes are composed of lipids, carbohydrates and proteins

3. The actual composition differs from tissue to tissue

4. Among the lipids, amphipathic lipids (containing hydrophobic and hydrophilic groups) namely phospholipids, glycolipids and cholesterol are found in the membrane

5. The biological membranes have a thickness of 5 to 8 nm

6. A membrane is essentially composed of a lipid bilayer

7. Membrane proteins are categorized into 2 groups

a) Extrinsic proteins – these are peripheral membrane proteins which are loosely held to the surface of the membrane and they can be easily separated eg. Cytochrome C of the mitochondria

b) Intrinsic proteins – these are integral proteins which are tightly bound to the lipid bilayer and can be separated only by the use of detergents or organic solvents eg. hormone receptors and cytochrome

8. The membrane is asymmetric due to the irregular distribution of proteins

9. The lipid and protein subunits of the membrane give an appearance of mosaic or ceramic tile

10. Unlike a fixed ceramic tile the membrane changes; hence the structure of the membrane is considered as fluid mosaic

FLUID MOSAIC MODEL

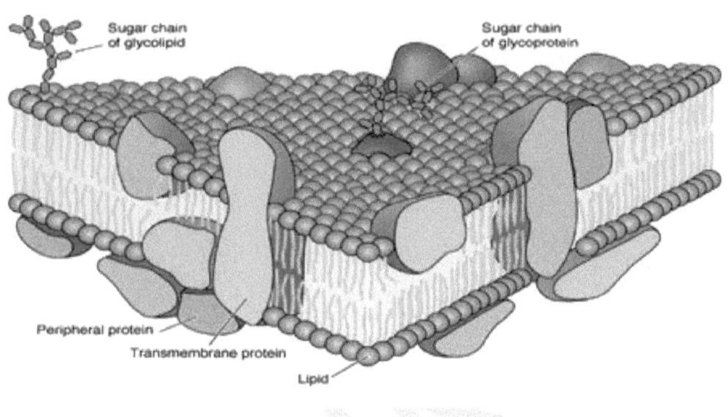

FLUID MOSAIC MODEL

Q 2. FUNCTIONS OF CELL MEMBRANE .

= **FUNCTIONS OF CELL MEMBRANE .**

1. It separates and protects the cell from the external hostile environment

2. The plasma membrane provides a connecting system between the cell and its environment

3. It acts as a semi permeable membrane

4. Absorptive function

5. Excretory function

6. Exchange of gases

7. Maintenance of size and shape of the cell .

Q 3.What are blood buffers? Explain their role in maintaining blood Ph.

==

CHAPTER FOURTEEN

COMPOSITION AND METABOLISM OF CARBOHYDRATES

Q 1.Classify carbohydrates with suitable examples .

= **DEFINITION OF CARBOHYDRATES**

Carbohydrates may be defined as polyhydroxy aldehydes or ketones or compounds which produce them on hydrolysis

CLASSIFICATION OF CARBOHYDRATES

Carbohydrates are classified into 3 groups:

1. Monosaccharides
2. Oligosaccharides
3. Diasaccharides
3. Polysaccharides

MONOSACCHARIDES

1. Monosaccharides are the simplest group of carbohydrates and are referred to as simple sugars
2. They cannot be further hydrolysed
3. The monosaccharides are divided into different categories depending on the functional group and the number of carbon atoms
4. When the functional group in monosaccharides is an aldehyde, they are known as aldoses e.g. glyceraldehyde, glucose
5. When the functional group is a keto group, they are known as ketoses e.g. dihydroxyacetone, fructose

6. Based on the number of carbon atoms, the monosaccharides are regarded as trioses (3C), tetroses (4C), pentoses (5C), hexoses (6C) and heptoses (7C).

OLIGOSACCHARIDES

1. Oligosaccharides contain 2 to 10 monosaccharide molecules which are liberated on hydrolysis

2. Based on the number of monosaccharide units present the oligosaccharides are further subdivided as –

a) Disaccharides (2) – e.g. Maltose

b) Trisaccharides (3) – e.g. Raffinose

c) Tetrasaccharides (4) – e.g. Stachyose

d) Pentasaccharides (5) – e.g. Fondaparinux

DISACCHARIDES

1. Disaccharides are sugars which yield two molecules of the same or different molecules of monosaccharides on hydrolysis e.g. maltose, lactose and sucrose

2 Maltose yields two molecules of glucose on hydrolysis

3. Lactose yields one molecule of glucose and one molecule of galactose on hydrolysis

4. Sucrose yields one molecule of glucose and one molecule of fructose on hydrolysis

POLYSACCHARIDES

1. Polysaccharides are sugars which yield more than ten molecules of monosaccharides on hydrolysis

2. They are of two types

a) Homo-polysaccharides – they are polymers of the same monosaccharide units e.g. – starch, glycogen, inulin, dextrin, dextran and cellulose

b) Hetero-polysaccharides - they are polymers of different monosaccharide units or their derivatives.

They are also known as mucopolysaccharides or glycosaminoglycans (GAGS)

e.g. – keratan sulfate, chondroitin sulfate, heparin and hyaluronic acid

Q 2. WRITE DOWN THE FUNCTIONS OF CARBOHYDRATES

.

= **FUNCTIONS OF CARBOHYDRATES**

1. Carbohydrates are the most abundant dietary source of energy (4 C/gm)

2. Carbohydrates are the precursors for many organic compounds such as fats and amino acids

3. Carbohydrates participate in the structure of cell membrane

4. Carbohydrates play a role in cellular functions such as cell growth, adhesion and fertilization

5. Carbohydrates serve as the storage form of energy (glycogen) to meet the immediate energy demands of the body

6. Carbohydrate derivatives are used as drugs e.g. cardiac glycosides and antibiotics

7. Lactose is the principal sugar of milk in the lactating mammary gland

8. Carbohydrates are constituents of compound lipids and conjugated proteins

9. Heparin is an anti-coagulant

10. Hetero-polysaccharides form the ground substance of tissues

Q 3. Factors regulating blood sugar level .

= **REGULATION OF BLOOD GLUCOSE LEVEL**

Blood glucose level is regulated by the following hormones:

1. Insulin
2. Glucocorticoids
3. Growth hormone
4. ACTH
5. Epinephrine
6. Glucagon
7. Thyroid hormones

INSULIN

Insulin is secreted from the beta cells of the pancreas.

Insulin decreases blood glucose level by

1. It decreases the delivery of glucose from the liver to the blood
2. It increase glycolysis
3. It increases glycogenesis
4. It decreases glycogenolysis
5. It decreases gluconeogenesis

GLUCOCORTICOIDS

Glucocorticoids are secreted from the adrenal cortex

Glucocorticoids increase blood glucose level by:

1. They increase protein catabolism in the peripheral tissues and the amino acids formed are used for gluconeogenesis
2. They decrease the peripheral uptake of glucose
3. They decrease glycolysis
4. They increase gluconeogenesis

GROWTH HORMONE

Growth hormone is secreted from the anterior pituitary gland

Growth hormone increases the blood glucose level by:

1. It decreases the glucose uptake by certain tissues e.g. muscles
2. It increases gluconeogenesis

ACTH

Adreno cortico tropic hormone (ACTH) is secreted from the anterior pituitary gland

It increases the blood glucose level by:

1. It increases the secretion of glucocorticoids
2. It increases gluconeogenesis

EPINEPHRINE

Epinephrine is secreted from the adrenal medulla

Epinephrine increases the blood glucose level by:

1. It increases glycogenolysis in the liver and muscles
2. It increases ACTH formation
3. It increases gluconeogenesis
4. It inhibits the release of insulin from the pancreas

GLUCAGON

Glucagon is secreted from the alpha cells of the pancreas

Glucagon increases blood glucose level by:

1. It increases glycogenolysis in the liver

2. It increases gluconeogenesis

THYROID HORMONES

Thyroid hormone (T3 and T4) are secreted from the thyroid gland

They increase the blood glucose level by:

1. They cause destruction of insulin
2. They increase the absorption of glucose from the intestine
3. They increase gluconeogenesis
4. They increase protein catabolism in the peripheral tissues and the amino acids formed are used for gluconeogenesis
5. They increase glycogenolysis

Q 4. Explain Cori's cycle .

= **CORI'S CYCLE**

1. Muscles cannot convert glucose 6 phosphate to glucose due to absence of the enzyme glucose 6 phosphatase
2. Lactate formed in the muscles enters the blood and is carried to the liver where it is converted to glucose by gluconeogenesis
3. The glucose thus formed then enters the muscles
4. This cycle is called Cori's cycle

CORI'S CYCLE

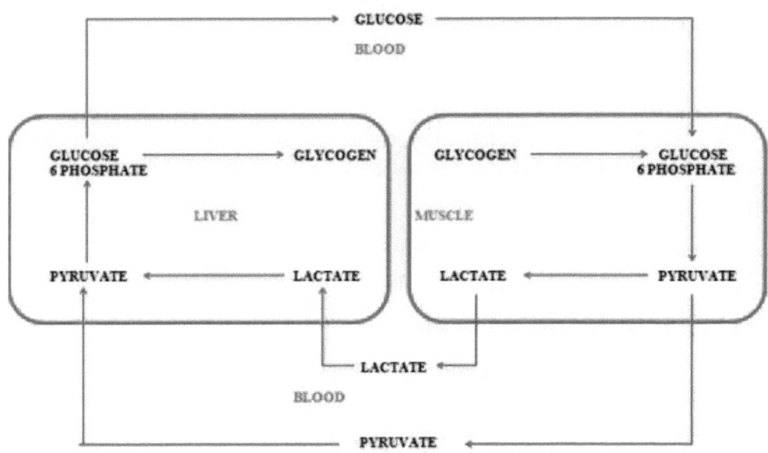

CORI'S CYCLE

Q 4. Describe the steps of TCA cycle. Add a note on its energetics.

= CHARACTERISTIC FEATURES OF KREBS CYCLE

1. Krebs cycle is also known as the citric acid cycle or tricarboxylic acid cycle (TCA cycle)
2. It is the final common pathway for the breakdown of carbohydrates, lipids and proteins
3. It takes place in the mitochondrial matrix
4. It takes place only in the presence of oxygen (aerobic conditions)
5. Absence of oxygen (anoxia) or partial deficiency of oxygen (hypoxia) causes total or partial inhibition of the cycle
6. NADH and $FADH_2$ formed in the Krebs cycle enter the electron transport chain and generate ATP's

7. Intermediates of Krebs cycle play a role in the synthesis of many important compounds such as non-essential amino acids, fatty acids, haeme, cholesterol and steroids.

REACTIONS OF KREBS CYCLE

1. Krebs cycle takes place in the mitochondria

2. Oxaloacetate combines with acetyl COA to form citrate in the first step of Krebs cycle

3. Citrate then undergoes a series of reactions to regenerate oxaloacetet

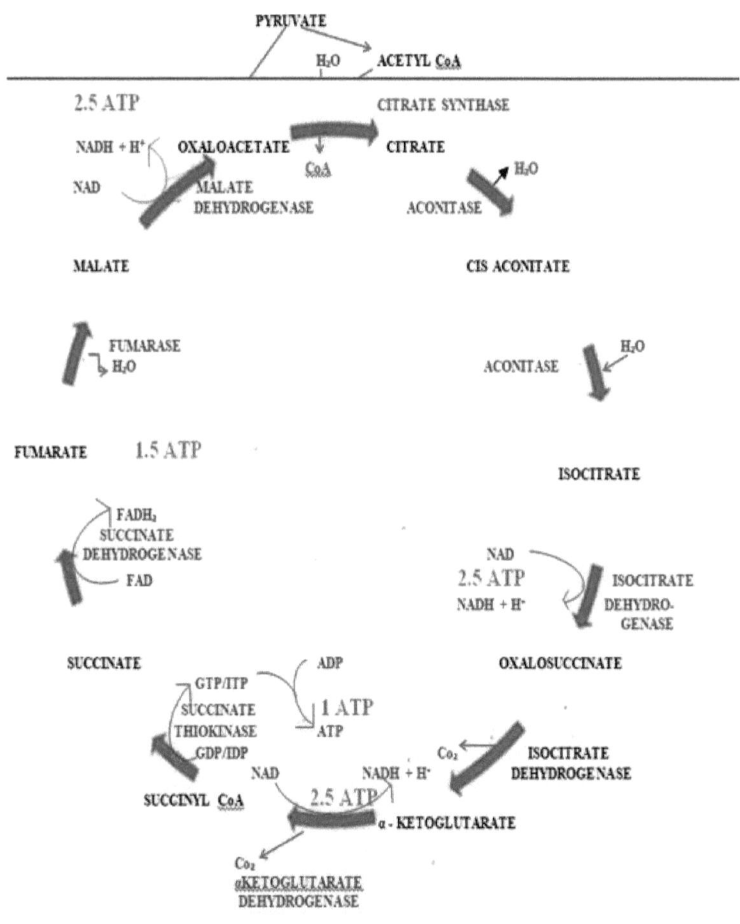

KREBS CYCLE

ENZYME	ATP GENERATED
ISOCITRATE DEHYDROGENASE	+ 5 ATP
ALPHA KETOGLUTARATE DEHYDROGENASE	+ 5 ATP
SUCCINATE THIOKINASE	+ 2 ATP
SUCCINATE DEHYDROGENASE	+3 ATP
MALATE DEHYDROGENASE	+ 5 ATP
NET GAIN	20 ATP

ENERGITICS OF KREBS CYCLE

Q 5. Explain glycolysis in detail with its energetics.

= GLYCOLYSIS

DEFINITION

The oxidation of glucose to pyruvate and lactate is called glycolysis

CHARACTERISTIC FEATURES OF GLYCOLYSIS

1. It is meant for the provision of energy
2. It is also called Embden Meyerhof Parnas (EMP) pathway
3. It occurs in all the tissues
4. Erythrocytes and brain derive energy mainly from glycolysis.
5. It can take place in both aerobic and anaerobic conditions.
6. Glycolysis takes place in the cytoplasm of the cell
7. It is important in skeletal muscles as glycolysis provides ATP even in the absence of oxygen, hence muscles can survive anoxic episodes
8. In fast growing cancer cells the rate of glycolysis is very high leading to the accumulation of lactic acid, causing acidosis.

The local acid environment is helpful in cancer therapy

9. Deficiency of certain enzymes (hexokinase and pyruvate kinase) of glycolysis can cause haemolytic anaemia.

REACTIONS OF GLYCOLYSIS

1. Glucose is freely permeable to liver cells
2. In the intestinal mucosa and kidney tubules glucose is taken up by active transport
3. In other tissues such as skeletal muscles, cardiac muscle, diaphragm and adipose tissue insulin facilitates the uptake of glucose
4. In aerobic conditions glucose is oxidized to pyruvic acid and in anaerobic conditions it is oxidized to lactic acid.

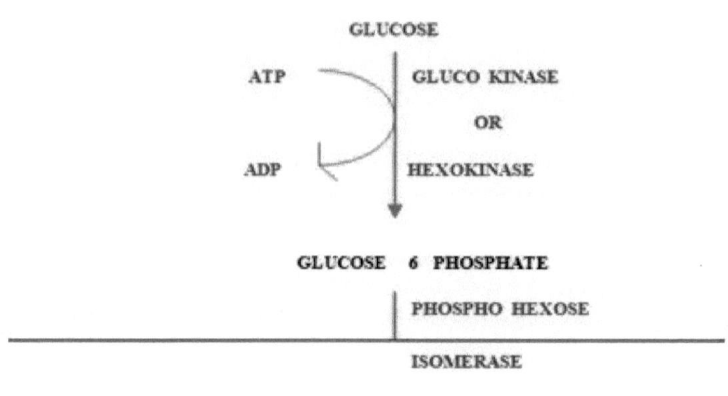

PHOSPHO HEXOSE

ISOMERASE

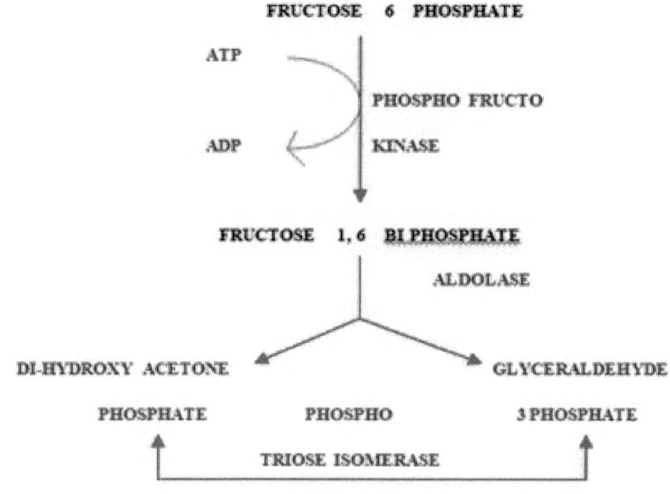

PHOSPHATE PHOSPHO 3 PHOSPHATE

TRIOSE ISOMERASE

GLYCOLYSIS 1

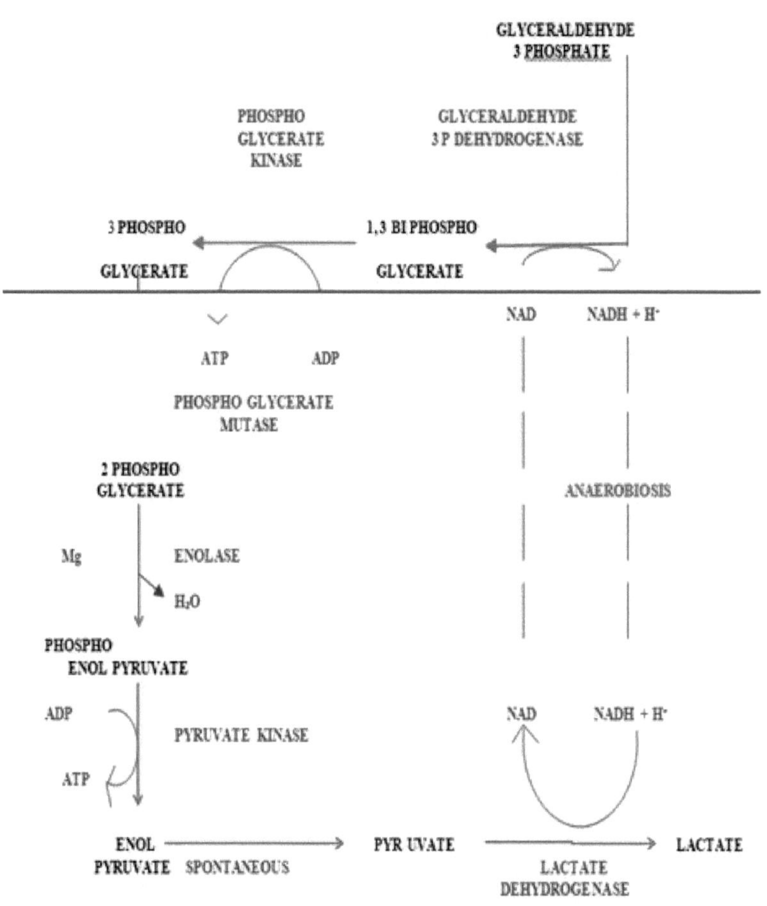

GLYCOLYSIS 2

ENZYME	ATP PRODUCTION
HEXOKINASE	- 1 ATP
PHOSPHOFRUCTOKINASE	- 1 ATP
GLYCERALDEHYDE 3 P DEHYDROGENASE	+ 5 ATP
PHOSPHOGLYCERATE KINASE	+ 2 ATP
PYRUVATE KINASE	+ 2 ATP
NET GAIN	7 ATP

ENERGITICS OF GLYCOLYSIS

Q 6. GLYCOGENESIS .

= GLYCOGENESIS / GLYCOGEN SYNTHESIS

DEFINITION

Glycogenesis is the formation of glycogen from glucose

SITES

1.Glycogenesis takes place in the liver and skeletal muscles

2. Storage capacity of glycogen in a normal adult man (70 kg) is

a) Liver – 70 to 110 grams

b) Skeletal muscles- 240 to 250 grams

REACTIONS OF GLYCOGENESIS

1. Glucose is phosphorylated to glucose 6 phosphate by the enzyme glucokinase

2. Glucose 6 phosphate is converted to glucose 1 phosphate by the enzyme phosphoglucomutase

3. Glucose 1 phosphate then reacts with UTP (uridine triphosphate) to form UDP glucose (uridine diphosphate glucose) under the influence of the enzyme UDPG pyrophosphorylase

4. C1 of the glucose of UDP glucose forms a glycosidic bond with the C4 of glucose of glycogen primer

5. The enzyme required is glycogen synthase and UDP is liberated in the reaction

6. A pre-existing glycogen primer must be present to initiate the reaction

7. In this way an existing glycogen chain can be repeatedly extended by one glucose unit at a time.

8. When the chain has lengthened to a minimum of 11 glucose units, branching enzyme transfers 6 glucose units, thus establishing a branch point in the molecule

9. The branches grow by further additions and further branching

10. 2 ATP's are required for glycogenesis.

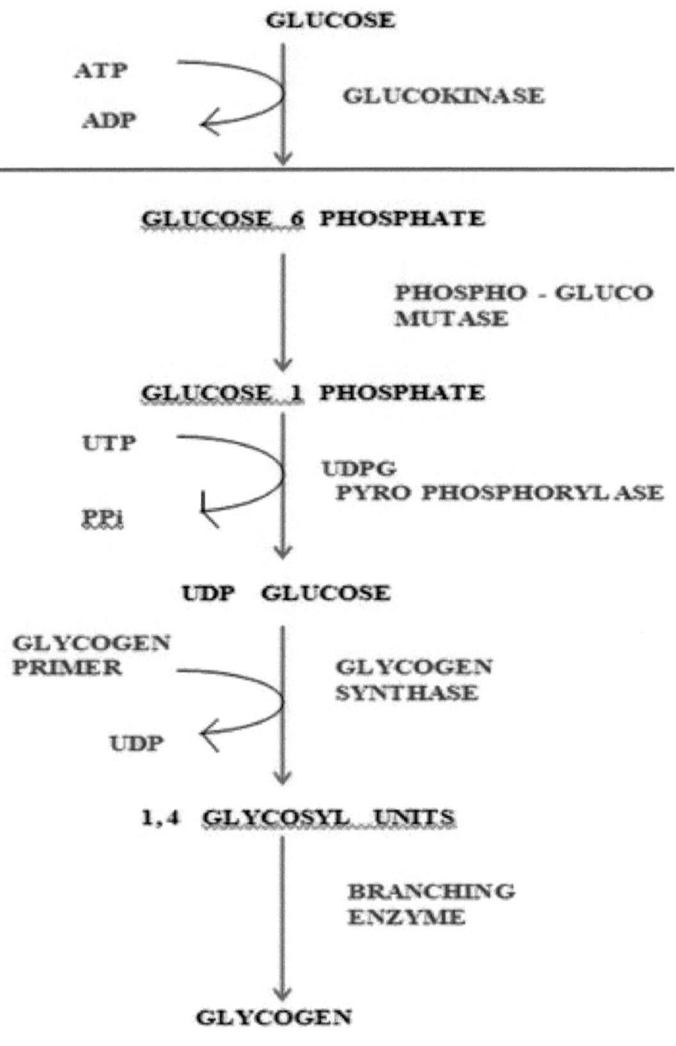

GLYCOGENESIS

Q 7. HMP SHUNT PATHWAY .

= CHARACTERISTIC FEATURES

1. HMP shunt (hexose mono phosphate shunt) is an alternate pathway for the oxidation of glucose

2. HMP shunt is also known as

a) Pentose phosphate pathway

b) Pentose cycle

c) Phospho-gluconate pathway

d) Warburg-Dickens-Lipmann pathway

e) Direct oxidative pathway

3. HMP shunt is a multi cyclic process

4. It is not meant to provide energy

5. It provides NADPH which is required for various metabolic pathways

6. It provides pentoses which are required for nucleic acid synthesis

7. Deficiency of the enzyme glucose 6 phosphate dehydrogenase (G6PD) of the HMP shunt pathway can cause haemolytic anemia

8. It occurs in certain specialized tissues e.g. liver, adipose tissue, RBC's, testes, ovary, adrenal cortex, lactating mammary gland, lens and cornea of the eye

9. Carbon dioxide is produced in this pathway

10. It takes place in the cytosol

11 ATP is required for HMP shunt pathway but ATP is not produced .

HMP 1
GLUCOSE
ATP
GLUCOKINASE
ADP
GLUCOSE 6 PHOSPHATE
NADP
GLUCOSE 6P
DEHYDROGENASE
NADPH + H+
6 PHOSPHOGLUCANOLACTONE
H_2O
GLUCANOLACTONE
HYDROLASE
6 PHOSPHOGLUCONATE
NADP
PHOSPHOGLUCONATE
DEHYDROGENASE
NADPH + H+
3 KETO 6 PHOSPHO GLUCONATE
CO_2
RIBULOSE 5 PHOSPHATE

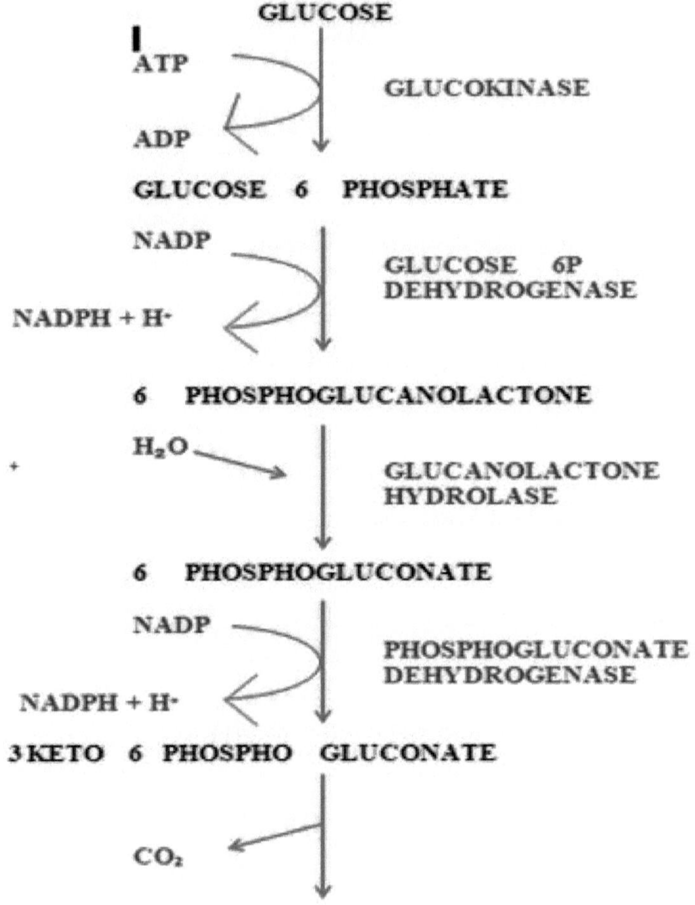

HMP 1

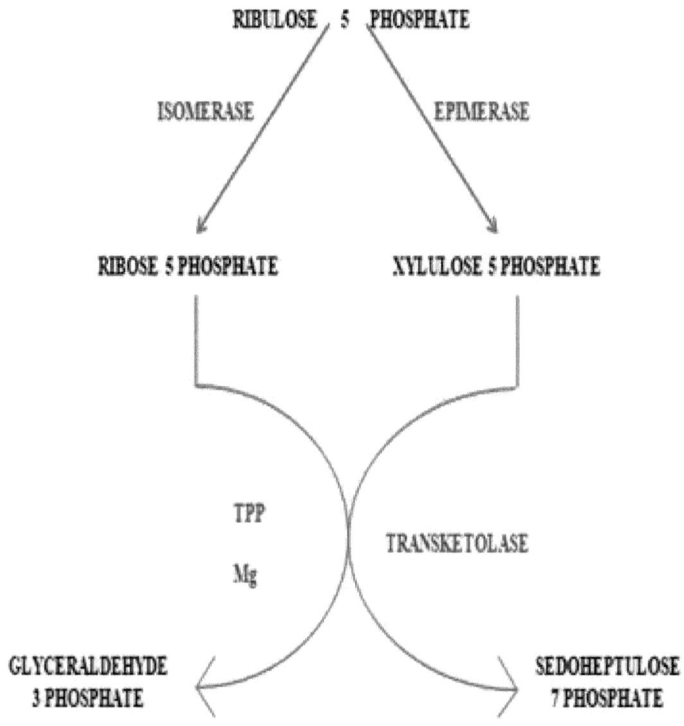

HMP 2

1.
GLYCERALDEHYDE 3PHOSPHATE
+
SEDOHEPTULOSE 7 PHOSPHATE
TRANSALDOLASE
ERYTHROSE 4 PHOSPHATE
+
FRUCTOSE 6 PHOSPHATE
2.
ERYHTROSE 4 PHOSPHATE
+
XYLULOSE 5 PHOSPHATE
TPP
Mg
TRANSKETOLASE
GLYCERALDEHYDE 3 PHOSPHATE
+
FRUCTOSE 6 PHOSPHATE

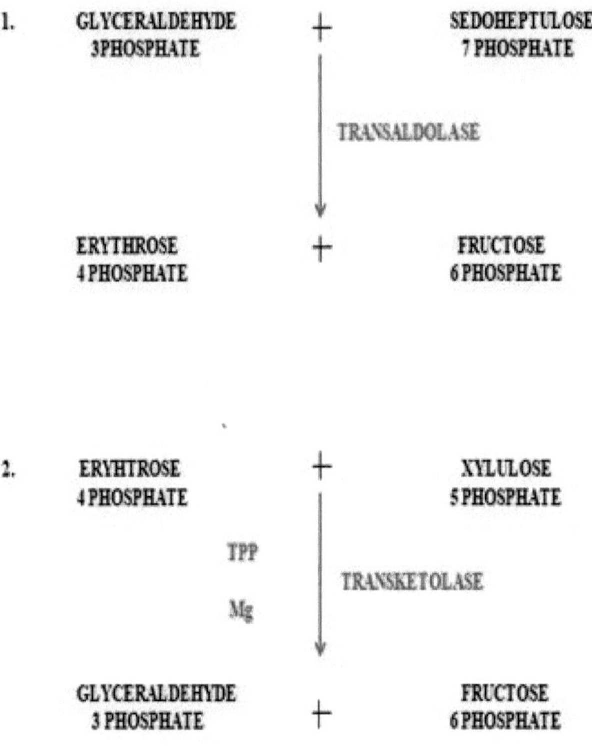

HMP 3

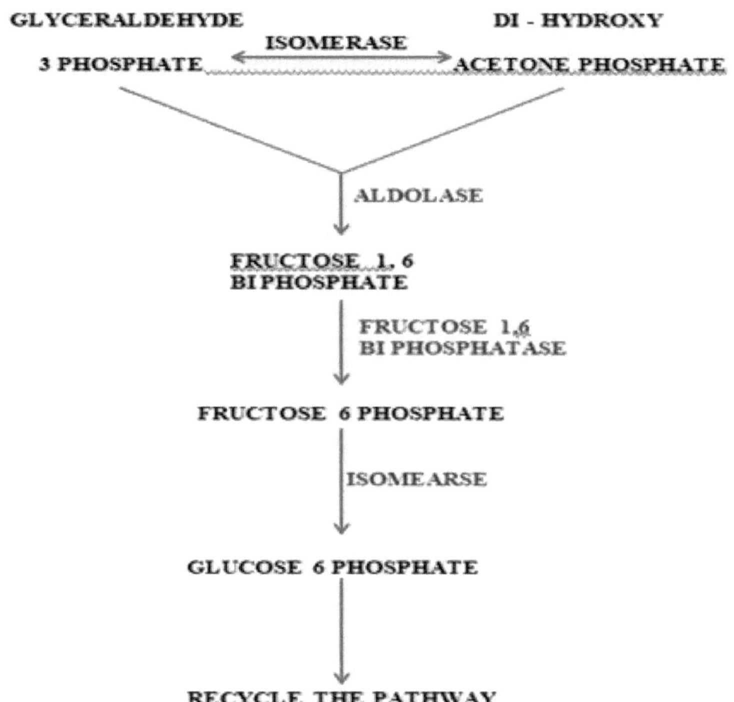

Q 8.GLUCONEOGENESIS .

= GLUCONEOGENESIS

DEFINITION

The formation of glucose from non carbohydrate sources is known as gluconeogenesis

1. Gluconeogenesis meets the requirement of glucose in the body when carbohydrates are not available in sufficient amounts in the diet

2. Glucose is the only source of energy for nervous tissue and erythrocytes

3. Glucose is required to maintain levels of intermediates of the Krebs cycle

4. It is a source of glycerol phosphate which is required for the adipose tissue

5. It is a precursor of milk sugar lactose for the lactating mammary gland

6. Glucose is the only source of energy for skeletal muscles in anaerobic conditions

SITES OF GLUCONEOGENESIS

Gluconeogenesis takes place in the liver and kidneys

CHAPTER FIFTEEN

COMPOSITION AND METABOLISM OF LIPIDS

Q 1. Classification of lipids .

= **DEFINITION OF LIPIDS**

Lipids are organic substances, relatively insoluble in water, soluble in organic solvents (alcohol, ether), related to fatty acids and utilized by living cells

CLASSIFICATION OF LIPIDS

Lipids are classified into the following groups

SIMPLE LIPIDS

These are esters of fatty acids with alcohol.

They are of two types:

a) Fats and oils (triacylglycerol)

These are esters of fatty acids with glycerol.

The difference between fat and oil is only physical.

Thus oil is a liquid while fat is a solid at room temperature

b) Waxes

These are esters of fatty acids with alcohol other than glycerol.

Cetyl alcohol is most commonly found in waxes

COMPLEX OR COMPOUND LIPIDS

These are esters of fatty acids with alcohols containing additional groups such as phosphate, nitrogenous base, carbohydrate and protein.

They are further divided as

PHOSPHOLIPIDS

These are lipids containing fatty acid, alcohol, phosphoric acid and nitrogenous base.

They are of the following types:

1. Glycero-phospholipids –

They contain glycerol as the alcohol e.g.

a) Phosphatidyl choline (lecithin)

b) Phosphatidyl ethanolamine (cephalin)

2. Sphingo-phospholipid

They contain sphingol as the alcohol. e.g.

Sphingomyelin

3. Phospho – inositide

They contain inositol as the alcohol. e.g.

Phosphatidyl inositol

GLYCOLIPIDS

These are lipids containing fatty acid, sphingol, nitrogenous base and carbohydrate e.g.

a) Cerebroside

b) Ganglioside

LIPOPROTEIN

They are a combination of lipids and proteins e.g.

a) Chylomicron

b) VLDL

c) LDL

d) HDL

Q 2. Functions of lipids

= **FUNCTIONS OF LIPIDS**

1. Lipids are constituents of membrane structure
2. Lipids regulate membrane permeability
3. Lipids are a source of fat soluble vitamins (A, D, E and K)
4. Lipids take part in regulation of cell metabolism
5. Lipids are an important source of energy (9.5 C/gm)

6. Lipids can be stored in the body in unlimited amounts

7. Lipids exert an insulating effect in the body

8. Lipids around internal organs like kidney may provide padding and protect the organ

9. Lipids are essential for proper functioning of the nervous system

10. Essential fatty acids (PUFA's) are required to be taken in the diet for normal health and growth

Q 3.Digestion and absorption of lipids .

= **Digestion of lipids :**

DIGESTION IN THE MOUTH

1. The enzyme lingual lipase is secreted from the dorsal surface of the tongue (Ebners gland).

2. It acts at a pH of 4 to 4.5.

3. It breaks down TG to fatty acid and glycerol

DIGESTION IN THE STOMACH

1. The enzyme gastric lipase acts at a pH of 7 to 8.

2. It requires calcium ion for its activity.

3. Activity of gastric lipase is seen when the intestinal contents are regurgitated into the stomach.

4. Fats delay the rate of emptying of the stomach and thus have high satiety value.

DIGESTION IN THE SMALL INTESTINE

1. Pancreatic juice enters the small intestine through the pancreatic duct and bile enters the small intestine through the bile duct.

2. Secretion of pancreatic juice is stimulated by the hormones secretin and Cholecystokinin – Pancreozymin (CCK-PZ)

3. Bile salts help in emulsification of fats (breakdown of fats into smaller units).

4. Pancreatic lipase acts at a pH of 6 and breaks down triglycerides into fatty acids and glycerol.

5. The enzyme cholesterol esterase breaks down cholesterol esters and phospholipase breaks down phospholipids.

ABSORPTION OF LIPIDS :

1. The resynthesized triglycerides in the intestinal epithelial cells cannot pass to lymphatics or to the portal blood as they are insoluble in water.

2. Triglycerides get covered with a layer of phospholipid, cholesterol and apoprotein to from the lipoprotein chylomicron.

3. Chylomicrons are soluble; they pass out through the intestinal epithelial cell and enter the blood and lymphatics.

Q 4. Classify lipoproteins with their functions .

= LIPOPROTEINS

DEFINITION

1. Lipoproteins are molecular complexes that consist of lipids and proteins.

2. They are conjugated proteins and they function as transport vehicles for lipids in the blood.

STRUCTURE OF LIPOPROTEINS

1. A lipoprotein consists of a neutral lipid core (triglyceride and cholesterol ester), surrounded by a shell of phospholipid, apoprotein and cholesterol.

2. The phospholipid and cholesterol are exposed on the surface of the lipoprotein so that the lipoprotein is soluble in aqueous solution

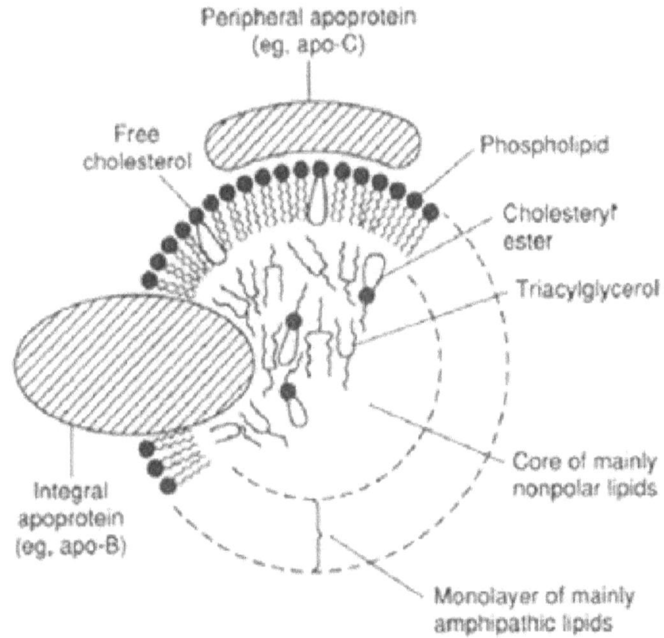

STRUCTURE OF LIPOPROTEINS

CLASSIFICATION OF LIPOPROTEINS

Lipoproteins can be classified by two methods:

1. Ultracentrifugation
2. Electrophoresis

CLASSIFICATION BY ULTRACENTRIFUGATION

By ultracentrifugation lipoproteins are classified as:

1. Chylomicrons – density lowest – floats
2. VLDL
3. LDL
4. HDL – density highest, sinks to the bottom (settles below)

BY ELECTROPHORESIS

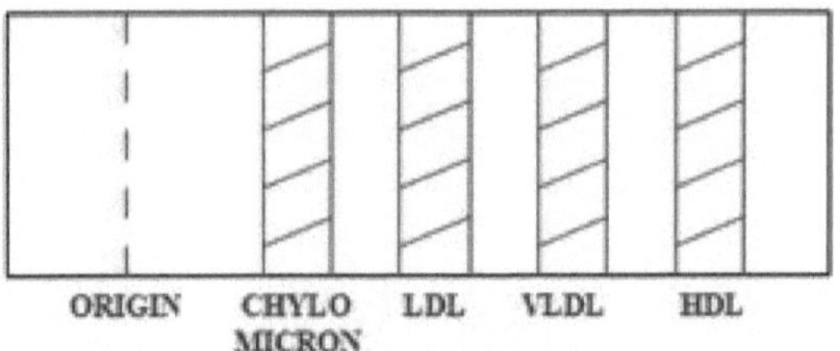

CLASSIFICATION BY ULTRACENTRIFUGATION

FUNCTIONS OF LIPOPROTEINS

CHYLOMICRONS

1. Chylomicrons are synthesised in the intestinal mucosal cells

2. They transport the exogenous triglycerides (triglycerides taken in the diet) from the intestine to the liver.

VLDL

1. VLDL are synthesised in the hepatic cells

2. VLDL transport the endogenous triglyceride (triglyceride synthesised in the body) from the liver to the peripheral tissues

IDL

1. VLDL is acted upon by the enzyme lipoprotein lipase which removes the triglycerides, to from IDL (intermediate density lipoprotein).

2. IDL loses some more triglyceride to form LDL

3. LDL is formed by the degradation of VLDL

4. LDL is very rich in cholesterol and cholesterol ester and poor in triglyceride

5. LDL transports cholesterol from the liver to the peripheral tissues

6. This is known as forward transport of cholesterol

7. Excessive deposition of cholesterol by LDL in the blood vessels can cause atherosclerosis; hence LDL is called BAD cholesterol

HDL

1. HDL is synthesised in the liver

2. HDL transports cholesterol from the peripheral tissues to the liver, where the cholesterol is degraded

3. This movement of cholesterol by HDL is called reverse transport of cholesterol

4. Since HDL helps in reducing blood cholesterol level, it is called GOOD cholesterol

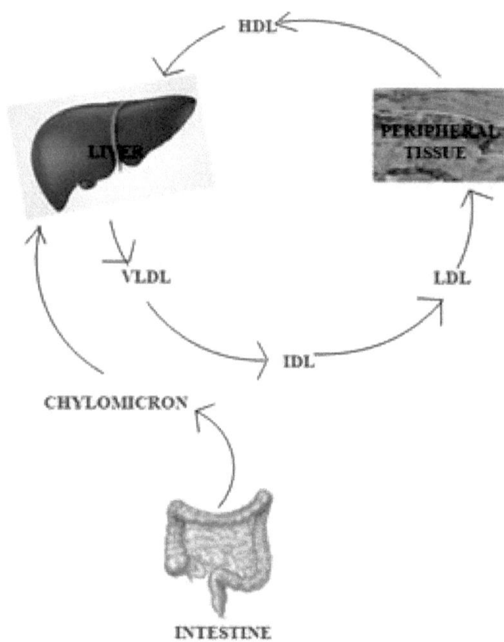

FUNCTIONS OF LIPOPROTEINS

Q 5. FUNCTIONS OF CHOLESTEROL .

= FUNCTIONS OF CHOLESTEROL

Cholesterol has four functions:

1. Synthesis of bile acids

2. Hormone synthesis
3. Vitamin D synthesis
4. Coprostanol synthesis

Q 6 Add a note on atherosclerosis.

= **ATHEROSCLEROSIS**

DEFINITION

Atherosclerosis is a complex disease characterised by thickening or hardening of the arteries due to accumulation of cholesterol in the inner arterial wall

MECHANISM OF ATHEROSCLEROSIS

1. Increased levels of cholesterol for prolonged periods will cause deposition of cholesterol in the subintimal region of the arteries
2. Coronary vessels and cerebral vessels are predominantly affected by this atherosclerotic process
3. LDL deposits the cholesterol in the macrophages, which become overloaded with cholesterol esters and are called "foam cells" and this leads to the formation of atherosclerotic plaques
4. The formation of atherosclerotic plaque leads to narrowing of the vessel wall
5. The blood flow through the narrow vessel lumen is more turbulent and there is tendency for clot formation
6. Finally a clot is formed, which occludes one of the major vessels
7. Thrombosis leads to ischaemia of the tissue supplied, due to decreased oxygen flow
8. Finally infarction or ischaemic death of the tissue occurs

DISORDERS THAT MAY CAUSE ATHEROSCLEROSIS

Certain diseases are associated with atherosclerosis, such as:

1. Diabetes mellitus
2. Hyper – lipoproteinemia
3. Nephrotic syndrome
4. Hypothyroidism

CAUSES OF ATHEROSCLEROSIS

Factors which may cause atherosclerosis are:

1. Obesity
2. High consumption of saturated fat
3. Excessive smoking
4. Lack of physical exercise
5. Stress

Q 8 Describe beta oxidation of palmitic acid. Add a note on its energetics.

= **BETA OXIDATION**

DEFINITION –

1.In beta oxidation the fatty acids are oxidised by the removal of 2 carbon atoms at a time.

2. The carbon atom in the beta position is attacked first; hence it is called beta oxidation

TISSUES IN WHICH BETA OXIDATION IS CARRIED OUT

1. Beta oxidation takes place in the liver, heart, kidney, testes and adipose tissue.

2. In cardiac muscle, 80 % of the energy is derived from beta oxidation

SITE OF BETA OXIDATION IN THE CELL

Beta oxidation takes place in the mitochondria

ACTIVATION OF FATTY ACIDS

1. Fatty acids are activated to acyl CoA by the enzyme thiokinase.

2. Two ATP's are required for the activation of fatty acids.

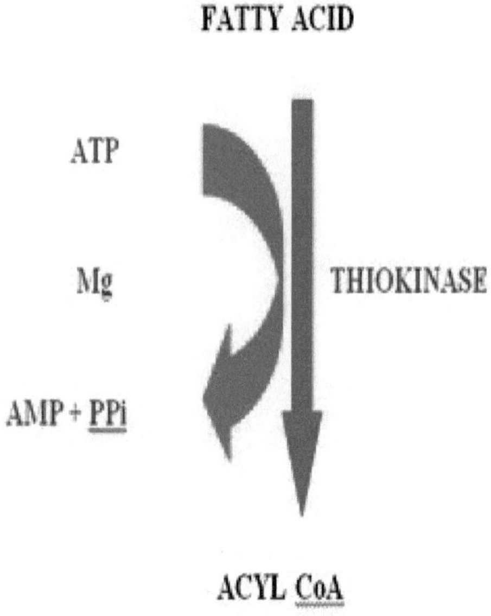

ROLE OF CARNITINE

1. Acyl CoA is formed in the cytosol whereas beta oxidation takes place in the mitochondrial matrix.

2. Acyl CoA cannot penetrate the mitochondrial membrane on its own.

3. Acyl CoA can penetrate the mitochondrial membrane only in combination with carnitine.

4. Carnitine is present in high concentration in the liver and muscles.

5. The normal blood level of carnitine is 7 to 14 micrograms %.

6. Carnitine is synthesised in the liver and kidneys from lysine and methionine.

7. Carnitine acts as a carrier molecule or ferry boat and transports acyl CoA across the mitochondrial membrane.

8. The enzymes required are carnitine palmitoyl transferase 1 and 2.

ROLE OF CARNITINE

1. Acyl CoA is formed in the cytosol whereas beta oxidation takes place in the mitochondrial matrix.

2. Acyl CoA cannot penetrate the mitochondrial membrane on its own.

3. Acyl CoA can penetrate the mitochondrial membrane only in combination with carnitine.

4. Carnitine is present in high concentration in the liver and muscles.

5. The normal blood level of carnitine is 7 to 14 micrograms %.

6. Carnitine is synthesised in the liver and kidneys from lysine and methionine.

7. Carnitine acts as a carrier molecule or ferry boat and transports acyl CoA across the mitochondrial membrane.

8. The enzymes required are carnitine palmitoyl transferase 1 and 2.

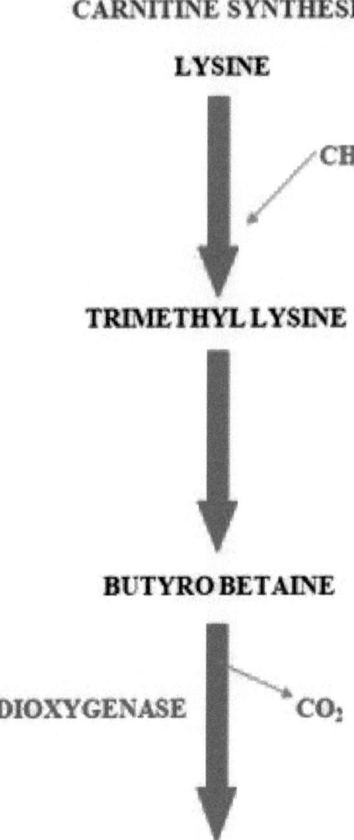
CARNITINE SYNTHESIS
LYSINE
CH3
TRIMETHYL LYSINE
BUTYRO BETAINE
DIOXYGENASE
CO2
CARNITINE

ROLE OF CARNITINE

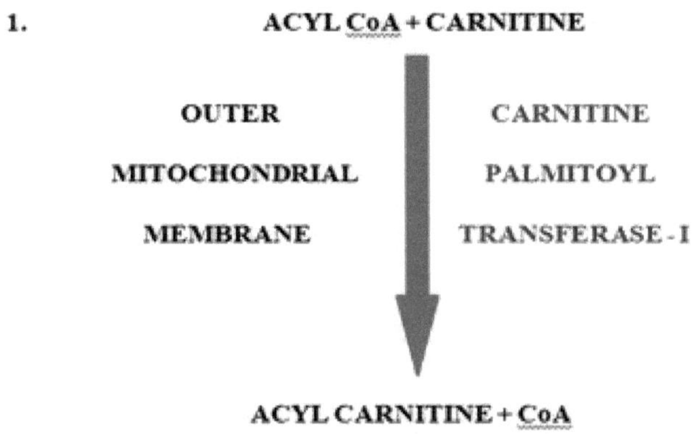

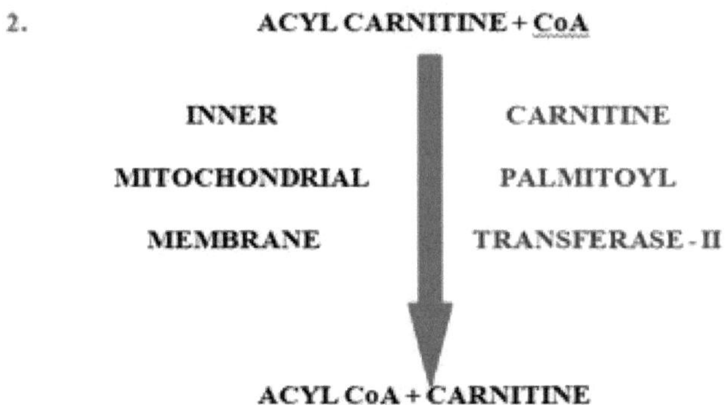

REACTIONS OF BETA OXIDATION

1. The end products of beta oxidation are acyl CoA and acetyl CoA.

2. The acyl CoA enters beta oxidation cycle again and the acetyl CoA enters the Krebs cycle where it oxidised to carbon dioxide and water.

BETA OXIDATION

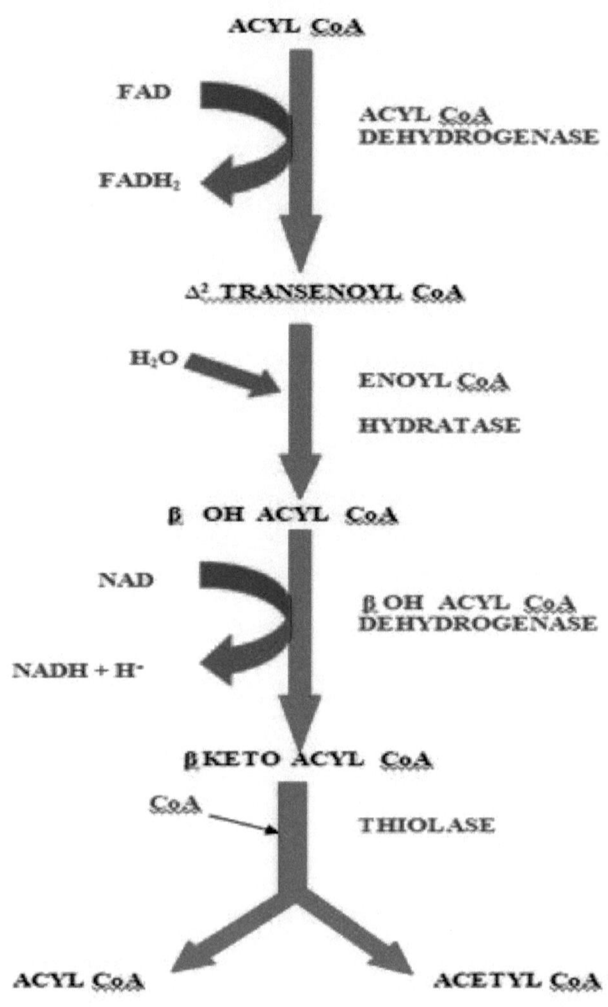

BETA OXIDATION

Palmitic acid is $C_{15}H_{31}COOH$.

2. Hence for complete beta oxidation it has to undergo 7 cycles producing 7 acetyl CoA.

3. One acetyl CoA is produced extra in the last cycle.

4. Hence the total acetyl CoA produced by beta oxidation of palmitic acid is 8.

ENERGITICS OF BETA OXIDATION

1. 4 ATP's are generated in each cycle of beta oxidation – 2.5 from NADH and 1.5 from $FADH_2$.

2. Hence 7 cycles will generate 28 ATP's.

3. 8 acetyl CoA when oxidised in the Krebs cycle will generate 80 ATP's.

4. Hence 108 ATP's (28 + 80) are generated.

5. 2 ATP's are required for activation of fatty acids.

6. Hence net generation of ATP's is 106.

CHAPTER SIXTEEN

COMPOSITION AND METABOLISM OF AMINO ACIDS AND PROTEINS

Q 1. Define proteins, classify them giving suitable examples.

= **PROTEINS**

DEFINITION

Proteins are polymers of amino acids.

They are the fundamental structural components of the body

CLASSIFICATION OF PROTEINS

Proteins can be classified in four ways

1. Classification based on shape and size
2. Functional classification
3. Classification based on chemical nature and solubility
4. Nutritional classification

CLASSIFICATION ON THE BASIS OF SHAPE AND SIZE

On the basis of shape and size proteins are classified into 2 types – fibrous and globular

FIBROUS PROTEINS

When the axial ratio of length to width of a protein molecule is more than 10, it is called a fibrous protein eg – keratin and collagen

GLOBULAR PROTEINS

When the axial ratio of length to width of a protein molecule is less than 10, it is called globular protein eg – haemoglobin and ribonuclease

FUNCTIONAL CLASSIFICATION OF PROTEINS

Based on the functions they perform, proteins are classified as

1. Structural proteins – they are involved in formation of structures of the body e.g. - keratin of hair and nail and collagen of bone

2. Enzyme proteins – all enzymes are protein in nature e.g. – hexokinase, pepsin

3. Transport proteins – proteins involved in transport of substances e.g. –

a) Haemoglobin transports oxygen

b) Albumin transports bilirubin

4. Hormonal proteins- some of the hormones are protein in nature e.g. Insulin and growth hormone

5. Contractile proteins – proteins which take part in muscle contraction. e.g. – Actin and myosin

6. Storage proteins – proteins involved in storage of substances e.g. – Ferritin stores iron

7. Genetic proteins – proteins involved in genetic function e.g. – Nucleoprotein

8. Defence proteins – proteins involved in defence function e.g. – Immunoglobulins

9. Receptor proteins – protein which act as receptors e.g. – Cytokine receptor, integrin

10. Respiratory proteins – proteins involved in the function of respiration e.g. – Haemoglobin and cytochrome

CLASSIFICATION BASED ON CHEMICAL NATURE AND SOLUBILITY

According to this proteins are classified into 3 groups – simple, conjugated and derived

SIMPLE PROTEINS

These are proteins which on complete hydrolysis yield only amino acids.

e.g.

1. Protamine – they are small molecules rich in arginine
2. Histones – they are found in association with DNA
3. Albumin – normal serum level is 3.5 to 5 gm %
4. Globulin – normal serum level is 1.8 to 3.6 gm %
5. Gliadin – it is rich in proline

NUTRITIONAL CLASSIFICATION OF PROTEINS

From the nutritional point of view proteins are classified as

1. Complete proteins
2. Partially incomplete proteins
3. Incomplete proteins

COMPLETE PROTEINS

These proteins have all the essential amino acids in the required proportions by the human body to promote good growth e.g. egg albumin and milk casein

PARTIALLY INCOMPLETE PROTEIN

These proteins are partially lacking one or more essential amino acids and hence can promote moderate growth e.g. – wheat and rice proteins (lack lysine and threonine)

INCOMPLETE PROTEINS

These proteins completely lack one or more essential amino acids, hence do not promote growth at all e.g. – gelatin (lacks tryptophan), maize/corn (lacks tryptophan and lysine)

Q 2. Transamination reactions .

= **TRANSAMINATION**

DEFINITION

Transamination is a reaction in which the amino group of one amino acid is transferred to a keto acid, resulting in the formation of a new amino acid and a new keto acid

CHARACTERISTIC FEATURES

1. Transamination is a reversible reaction
2. It takes place in the liver, kidney, heart and brain
3. The enzyme required is called transaminase

4. Pyridoxine is required as a coenzyme for the reaction

5. While most amino acids can act as donors, the recipient keto acids may be alpha ketoglutarate, oxaloacetate or pyruvate

6. All the recipient keto acids are components of the Krebs cycle

7. The amino acids which do not take part in transamination are lysine, threonine, proline and hydroxyproline

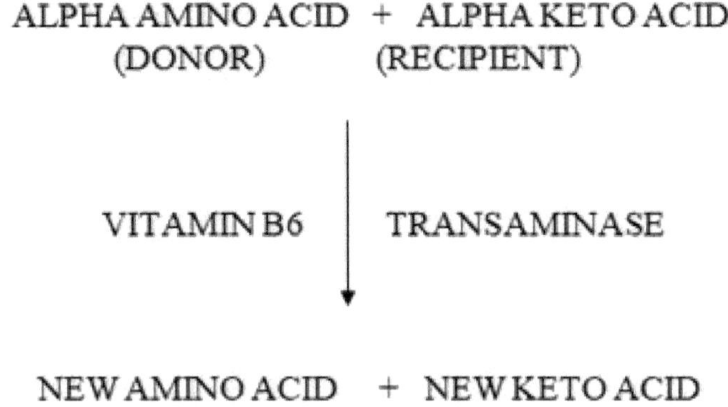

Q 3. UREA CYCLE

= **DEFINITION**

The removal of excess ammonia derived from amino acid catabolism is accomplished by the production of urea, which is excreted in the urine.

This cycle is known as urea cycle

CHARACTERISTIC FEATURES

1. It is also known as Krebs-Henseleit cycle

2. Urea cycle takes place in the liver, kidney, intestine and brain.

3. Urea synthesis does not occur in the brain, kidney or intestine due to absence of some enzmyes

4. Urea formation takes place only in the liver

5. Urea cycle takes place partly in the mitochondria and partly in the cytoplasm

6. One molecule of ammonia and one molecule of carbon dioxide are converted to one molecule of urea in each turn of the cycle and ornithine is regenerated at the end

7. Each turn of the urea cycle requires 4 ATP's.

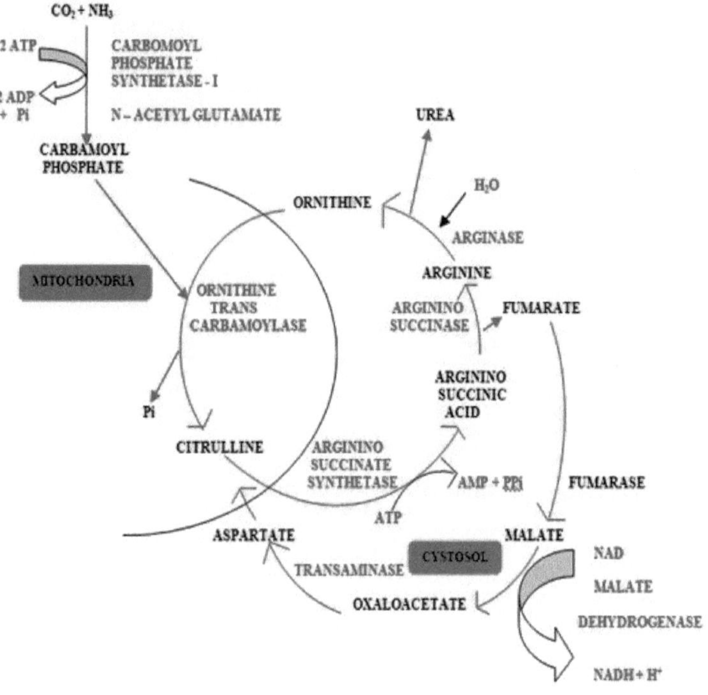

UREA CYCLE

Importance :

1. The major biological role of urea cycle is detoxification of ammonia

2. Toxic ammonia is converted to non toxic urea and excreted in the urine

3. The normal blood ammonia level is 40 to 70 micrograms %

4. Hyperammonemia occurs due to cirrhosis of the liver or genetic defects in urea cycle enzymes.

Q 3.Write a note on transamination and deamination reactions in protein metabolism.

= **TRANSAMINATION**

DEFINITION

Transamination is a reaction in which the amino group of one amino acid is transferred to a keto acid, resulting in the formation of a new amino acid and a new keto acid

CHARACTERISTIC FEATURES

1. Transamination is a reversible reaction
2. It takes place in the liver, kidney, heart and brain
3. The enzyme required is called transaminase
4. Pyridoxine is required as a coenzyme for the reaction
5. While most amino acids can act as donors, the recipient keto acids may be alpha ketoglutarate, oxaloacetate or pyruvate
6. All the recipient keto acids are components of the Krebs cycle
7. The amino acids which do not take part in transamination are lysine, threonine, proline and hydroxyproline.

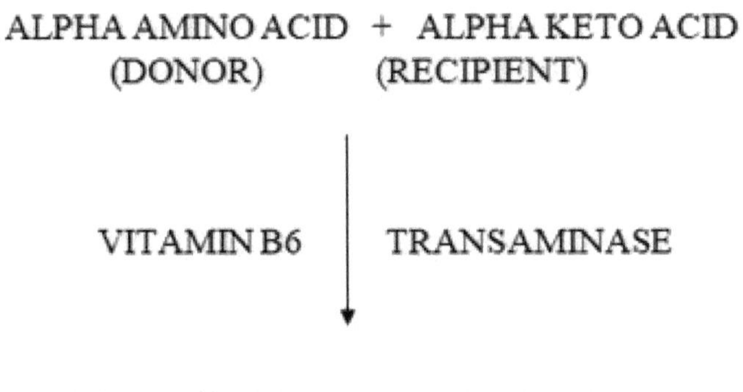

TRANSAMINATION

DEAMINATION

DEFINITION

The removal of amino group from the amino acid is known as deamination

TYPES

It can be of two types

1. Oxidative deamination
2. Non oxidative deamination

OXIDATIVE DEAMINATION

1. It is a process in which ammonia is removed from the amino acid
2. It takes place in the liver and kidney
3. The enzyme required is amino acid oxidase
4. Amino acid is converted to imino acid which then forms keto acid and ammonia is eliminated
5. Hydrogen peroxide is formed, which is toxic to the cells and is immediately broken down by the enzyme catalase
6. It does not play a major role in the formation of ammonia.

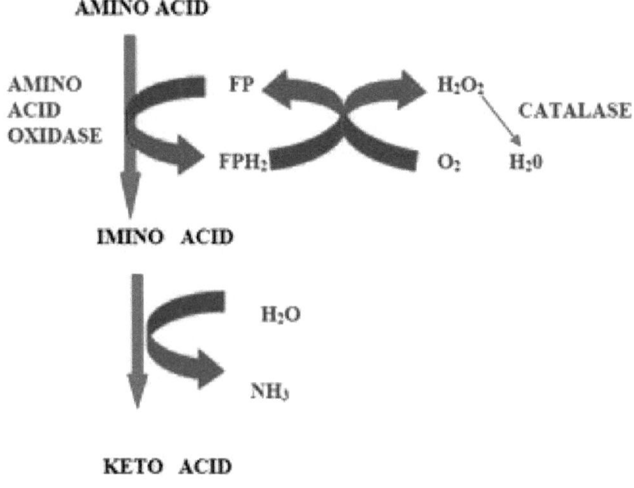

DEFINITION

Q 5. Define oxidative and non- oxidative deamination.

= DEAMINATION

DEFINITION

The removal of amino group from the amino acid is known as deamination

TYPES

It can be of two types

1. Oxidative deamination
2. Non oxidative deamination

OXIDATIVE DEAMINATION

1. It is a process in which ammonia is removed from the amino acid
2. It takes place in the liver and kidney
3. The enzyme required is amino acid oxidase
4. Amino acid is converted to imino acid which then forms keto acid and ammonia is eliminated
5. Hydrogen peroxide is formed, which is toxic to the cells and is immediately broken down by the enzyme catalase
6. It does not play a major role in the formation of ammonia.

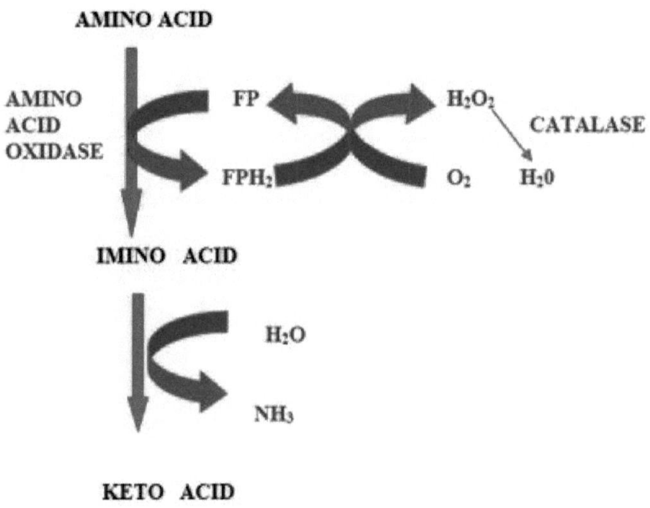

OXIDATIVE DEAMINATION

NON OXIDATIVE DEAMINATION

1. Certain amino acids can be non-oxidatively deaminated by specific enzymes to form ammonia
2. It does not play a major role in ammonia formation.

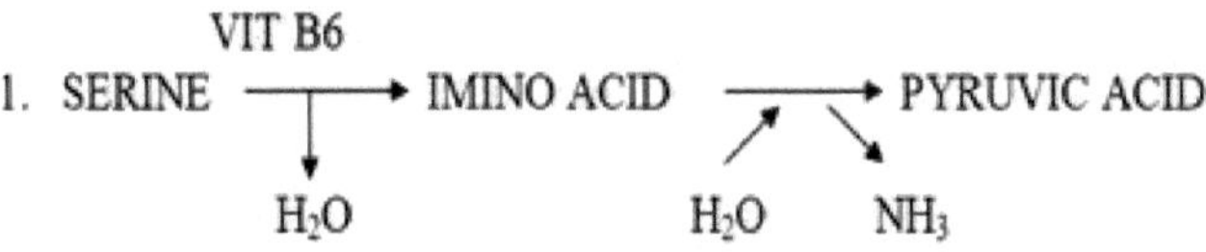

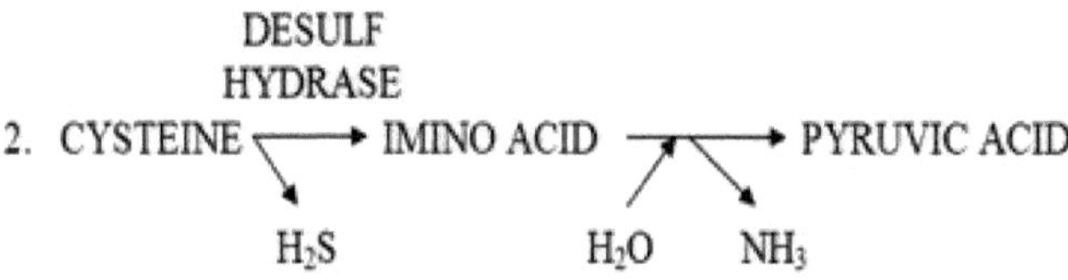

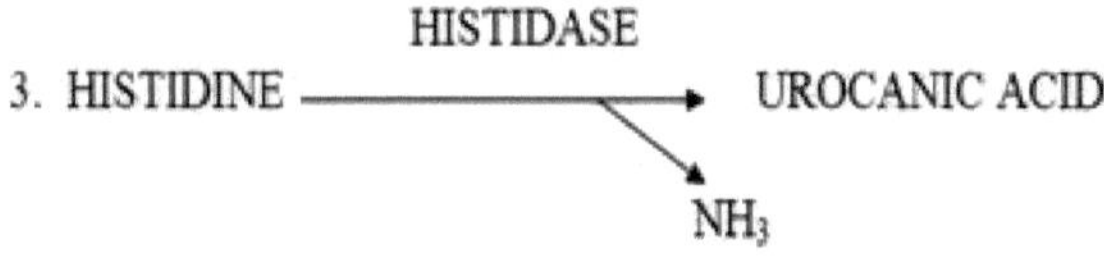

1

NON OXIDATIVE DEAMINATION

CHAPTER SEVENTEEN

ENZYMES

Q 1. Classification of enzymes with suitable examples .

= **DEFINITION**

Enzymes may be defined as biocatalysts synthesized by living cells.

They are protein in nature, colloidal, thermo labile in character and specific in action

CLASSIFICATION OF ENZYMES

1. In order to have uniformity in identification of enzymes, the International Union of Biochemistry (IUB) adopted a nomenclature system based on chemical reaction type and reaction mechanism

2. According to this system the enzymes are grouped in six classes

3. The enzymes are classified as

a) Oxidoreductases

b) Transferases

c) Hydrolases

d) Lyases

e) Isomerases

f) Ligases

OXIDOREDUCTASES

1. These enzymes are involved in oxidation reduction reactions

2. The reaction is

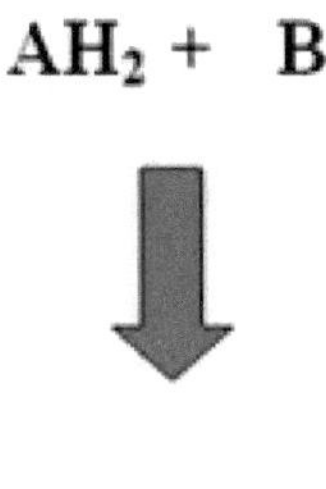

A + BH2

3. Examples of oxidoreductases:

a) Alcohol dehydrogenase

b) Acyl CoA dehydrogenase

c) Glyceraldehyde 3 phosphate dehydrogenase

d) Cytochrome oxidase

e) Amino acid oxidase

f) Xanthine oxidase

g) Glutathione reductase

h) Catalase

TRANSFERASES

1. Enzyme that catalyze the transfer of a particular group from one substrate to another

2. The reaction is

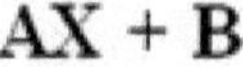

A + BX

3. Examples of transferases are:

a) Aspartate transaminase

b) Ornithine carbamoyl transferase

c) Methyl transferase

d) Phosphorylase

e) Hexokinase

HYDROLASES

1. These are enzymes which bring about hydrolysis of various compounds

2. The reaction is

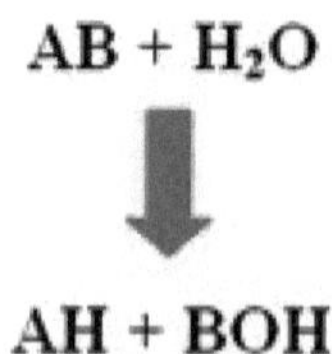

HYDROLASES

3. Examples of hydrolases are:

a) Alkaline phosphatase

b) Glucose 6 phosphatase

c) Lipase

d) Choline esterase

e) Urease

f) Amylase

g) Pepsin

h) Trypsin

LYASES

1. Enzymes that help in the removal of a small molecule from a large substrate

2. The reaction is

A X + B Y

LYASES

3. Examples of lyases are:

a) Histidase

b) Argininosuccinase

c) Aldolase

d) Fumarase

ISOMERASES

1. These are enzymes involved in isomerization reactions

2. The reaction is

A---> A'

3. Examples of isomerases are:

a) Phospho triose isomerase
b) Retinol isomerase
c) Maleyl acetoacetate isomerase
d) UDPG epimerase
e) Racemase

LIGASES

1. These are enzymes involved in joining together of 2 substrates
2. The reaction is

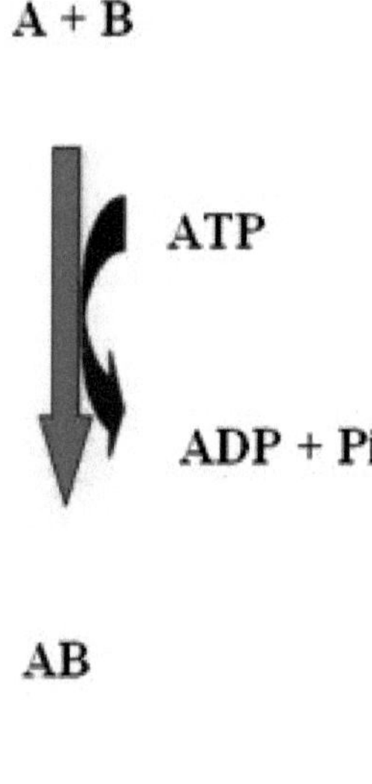

LIGASES

3. Examples of ligases are:

a) Glutamine synthetase
b) Glycogen synthetase
c) Delta ALA synthase
d) Acetyl CoA carboxylase
e) Succinate thiokinase f) DNA ligase

Q 2. Define enzymes. Explain in detail factors affecting enzyme action.

= **DEFINITION**

Enzymes may be defined as biocatalysts synthesized by living cells.

They are protein in nature, colloidal, thermo labile in character and specific in action

FACTORS AFFECTING ENZYME ACTION

The factors which affect enzyme action are:

1. Temperature
2. pH
3. Enzyme concentration
4. Product concentration
5. Substrate concentration
6. Coenzymes
7. Metal ion activators
8. Inhibitors

EFFECT OF TEMPERATURE

1. Each enzyme is most active at a particular temperature known as optimum temperature
2. Optimum temperature of most enzymes is in the range of 35 to 40 degrees Celsius
3. Reaction velocity almost doubles with 10 degrees Celsius rise in temperature in many enzymes but a very great increase in temperature can cause denaturation of enzyme
4. Activity of the enzyme progressively decreases when the temperature of the reaction is below or above the optimum temperature
5. It shows a bell shaped curve

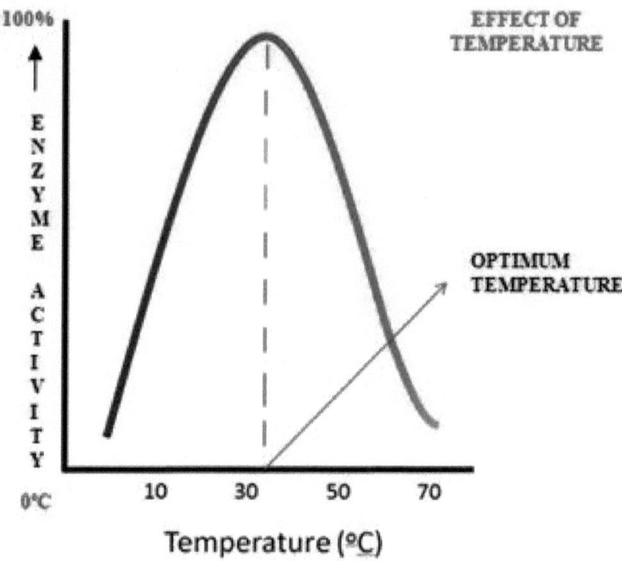

EFFECT OF TEMPERATURE

EFFECT OF pH

1. The enzymatic activity is optimum at a particular pH known as optimum pH
2. The optimum pH for most enzymes is in the range of 4 to 9
3. At a very low or very high pH the enzyme structure may be destroyed
4. It shows a bell shaped curve

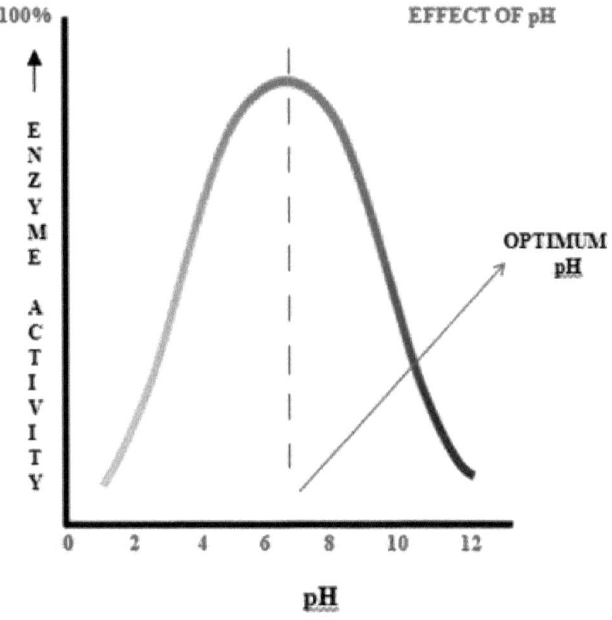

EFFECT OF pH .

EFFECT OF ENZYME CONCENTRATION

1. Velocity of the enzymatic reaction is directly proportional to the enzyme concentration

2. Providing more enzyme molecules enables the conversion of progressively larger number of substrate molecules into products

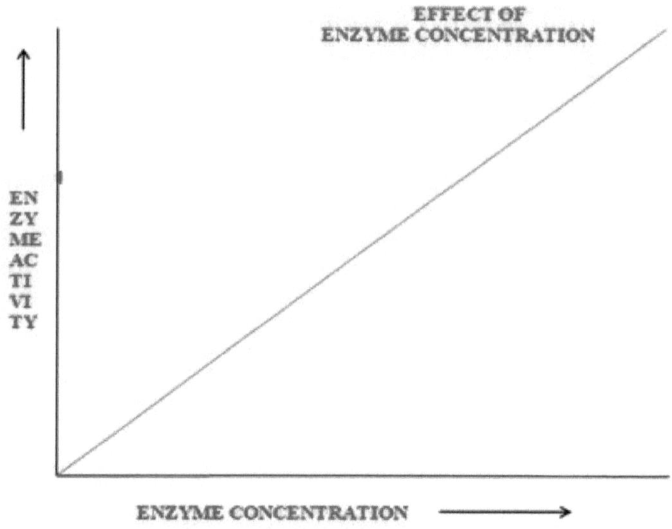

EFFECT OF ENZYME CONCENTRATION

EFFECT OF PRODUCT CONCENTRATION

1. Products formed as a result of reaction may accumulate and this excess of product may lower the reaction by occupying the active site of the enzyme

2. In certain conditions a high concentration of products may cause a reverse reaction forming back the substrate.

EFFECT OF SUBSTRATE CONCENTRATION

1. For a known quantity of enzyme, the reaction is directly proportional to the substrate concentration.

2. However this is true only upto a certain concentration after which the increasing concentration of substrate does not further increase the velocity of the reaction

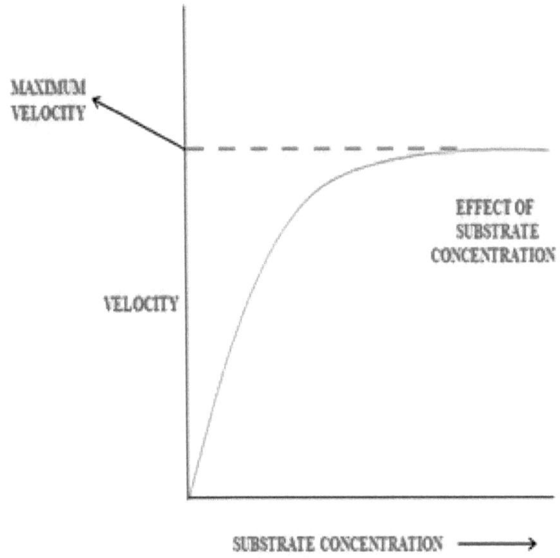

EFFECT OF SUBSTRATE CONCENTRATION

EFFECT OF COENZYME

1. Some enzymes require non protein, organic, low molecular weight substances known as coenzymes for their action

2. These enzymes cannot act in the absence of coenzymes

3. Examples –

a) TPP is the coenzyme for transketolase enzyme.

b) NAD is the coenzyme for lactate dehydrogenase.

EFFECT OF METAL ION ACTIVATORS

1. Some enzymes require certain inorganic metallic cations for their optimum activity.

2. Examples

a) ATPase requires calcium

b) Enolase requires magnesium

c) Phenol oxidase requires copper

d) Pyruvate oxidase requires manganese

e) Xanthine oxidase requires molybdenum

f) Cytochrome oxidase requires iron

EFFECT OF ENZYME INHIBITORS

1. Enzyme inhibitor is defined as a substance which binds with the enzyme and brings about a decrease in the enzyme activity.

2. Examples -

a) Lactate dehydrogenase is inhibited by oxamate

b) HMG COA reductase is inhibited by HMG

c) Aconitase is inhibited by transaconitate

d) Succinate dehydrogenase is inhibited by malonate.

Q 3. Describe competitive and non- competitive inhibition of enzymes with their examples .

= COMPETITIVE INHIBITION

1. When the active site of the enzyme is occupied by a substance other than the substrate of the enzyme, its activity is inhibited.

2. This is known as competitive inhibition

3. It is a reversible type of inhibition

4. In competitive inhibition both ES and EI complexes are formed during the reaction

5. The affinity of the substrate for the enzyme is progressively decreased with the increase in concentration of the inhibitor, thus lowering the rate of enzymatic reaction

6. However, when the concentration of substrate is increased, the effect of inhibitor can be reversed, forcing it out of the EI complex

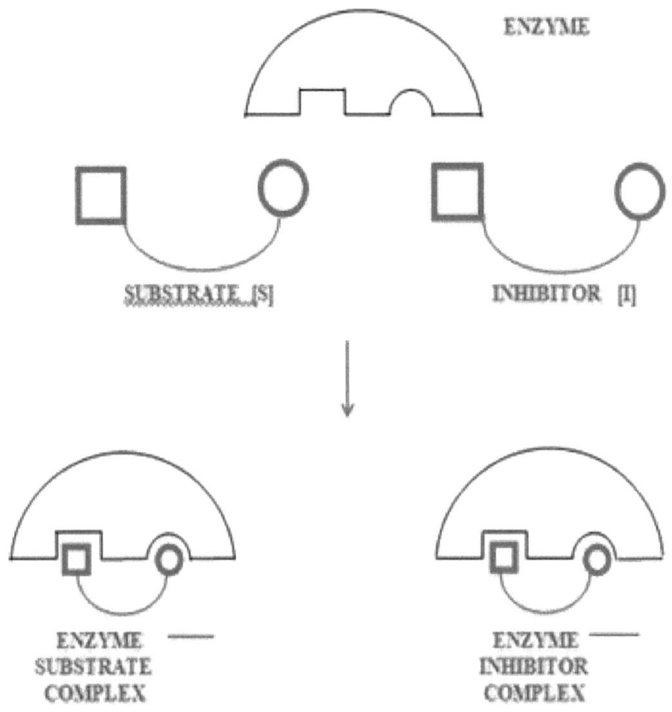

COMPETITIVE INHIBITION

CLINICAL IMPORTANCE OF COMPETITIVE INHIBITORS

1) Allopurinol

a) Enzyme – Xanthine oxidase

b) Substrate – Xanthine

c) Inhibitor – Allopurinol

d) Significance – Treatment of gout

2) Amphetamine

a) Enzyme - Monoamine oxidase

b) Substrate – Epinephrine

c) Inhibitor – Amphetamine

d) Significance – To elevate catecholamine levels

NON COMPETITIVE INHIBITION

1. This occurs when substances not resembling geometry of the substrate do not exhibit mutual competition.

2. The sites of attachment of the substrate and inhibitor are different

3. The inhibitor binds with a site on the enzyme other than the active site.

4. The inhibitor may combine with both free enzyme and ES complex.

5. There are 2 types of non competitive inhibition –

a) Reversible

b) Irreversible

6. Reversible non competitive inhibition

a) If the inhibitor can be removed from its site of binding without affecting the activity of the enzyme, it is called reversible non competitive inhibition.

b) Example – heavy metal ions (lead, silver, mercury) inhibit enzymes by binding with the cysteinyl sulfhydryl groups.

7. Irreversible non competitive inhibition

a) If the inhibitor can be removed from the site of binding only with the loss of enzymatic activity, it is called irreversible non competitive inhibition

b) Example – iodoacetate inhibits the enzyme glyceraldehyde 3 phosphate dehydrogenase

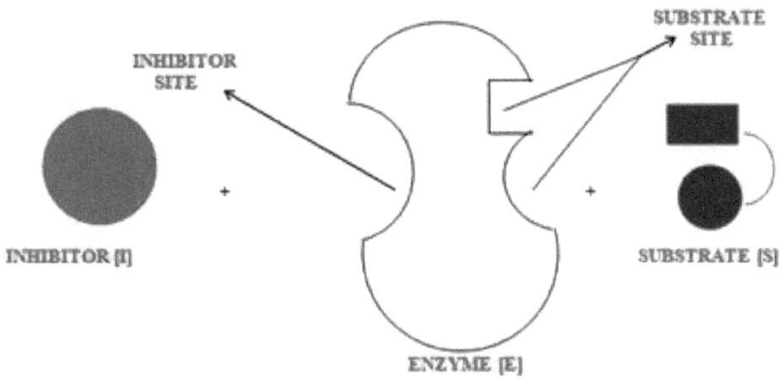

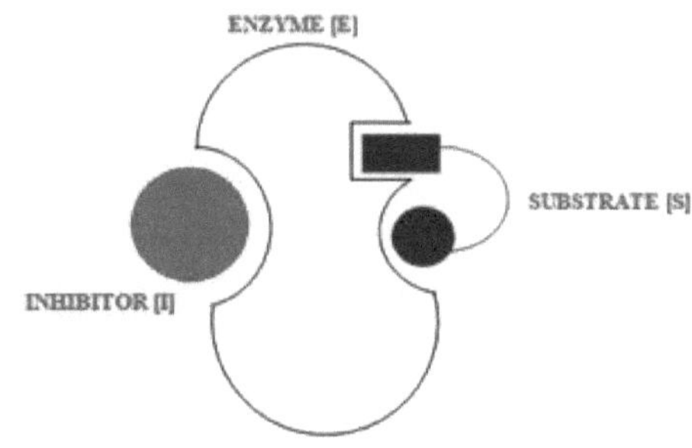

NON COMPETITIVE INHIBITION

CHAPTER EIGHTEEN

COMPOSITION OF VITAMINS

Q 1.Define and classify vitamins.

= **DEFINITION OF VITAMINS**

1. Vitamins are defined as organic compounds occurring in natural foods, which are required in minute amounts for normal growth, maintenance and reproduction

2. Chemically they were found to be amines and they were vital to life, hence Funk named them “vitamins”

Classification of vitamins

Fat-soluble vitamins

a. Vitamin A, D,E and K are know as fat or lipid – soluble vitamins.

n. Their availability in the diet, absorption and transport are associated with fat.

n. They are soluble in fats and oils and also the fat solvents (alcohol, acetone etc.)

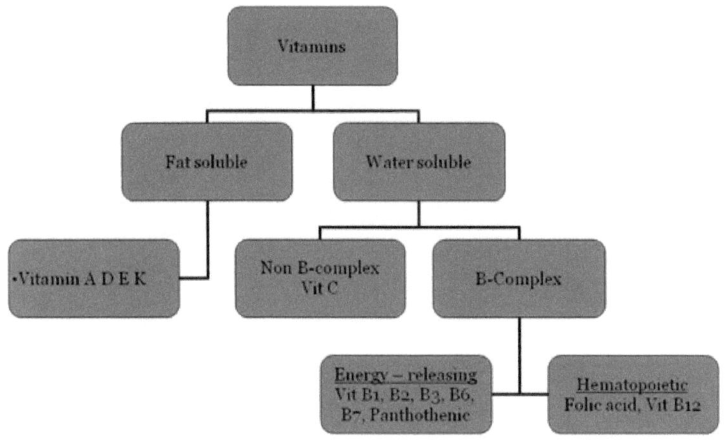

Classification of vitamins

They are stored in the liver and adipose tissue.

They are not readily excreted in urine. But with feceas via the enterohepatic circulation

Excess consumption may lead to accumulation and toxic effects.

Water soluble vitamins

Heterogeneous group of compounds since they differ chemically from each other.

Common character – solubility in water.

Readily excreted in urine and not toxic to body.

Not stored in large quantities in the body (except vitamin B12).

Stores depleted within weeks and deficiency symptoms results.

Hence need to be continuously supplied through the diet.

Q 2. Write sources, daily requirement, functions and deficiency manifestation of vitamin A

= INTRODUCTION

1. Vitamin A exists in three forms

a) Vitamin A alcohol – retinol

b) Vitamin A acid – retinoic acid

c) Vitamin A aldehyde – retinal

2. Vitamin A can also be formed from provitamins, known as carotenes

DAILY REQUIREMENT

4000 to 5000 IU

1 IU = 0.3 micrograms of retinol

DIETARY SOURCES

1. Animal sources – liver, kidney, egg yolk, milk, cheese, butter and cod liver oil

2. Vegetable sources – carotenes – carrots, spinach, pumpkins, mango and papaya

FUNCTIONS OF VITAMIN A

ROLE IN VISION is main function of vitamin A

1. Vitamin A is required for normal reproduction

2. Vitamin A is required for epithelialization and is essential to maintain healthy epithelial tissue.

3. Vitamin A is required for the construction of normal bone and teeth

4. Vitamin A is required for glycoprotein synthesis

5. Vitamin A is required for the synthesis of chondroitin sulfate

6. Vitamin A plays a role in cell differentiation and cell division

7. Vitamin A is involved in protein synthesis

8. Vitamin A plays a role in DNA metabolism

9. Carotenes function as antioxidants and reduce the risk of cancers initiated by free radicals

VITAMIN A DEFICIENCY

1. Retinol deficiency depresses the re-synthesis of rhodopsin and interferes with the function of rods resulting in night blindness

2. In Vitamin A deficiency sperm cells do not mature and in females there may be abortion.

3. In Vitamin A deficiency the skin becomes dry, scaly and rough. These changes are called keratinisation.

4. There is dryness of the conjunctiva and cornea, which is known as xerophthalmia.

5. White opaque spots, known as Bitots spots appear on the conjunctiva.

6. Cornea becomes keratinized, opaque, soft and ulcerated. This is known as keratomalacia.

7. Keratinization occurs in the mucous membrane of the respiratory tract leading to increased susceptibility to infection and lowered resistance to disease.

8. Vitamin A deficiency causes arrested bone development.

9. The teeth become unhealthy with chalky deposits on the surface.

Q 3 . Describe sources, recommended daily allowance, biological functions and deficiency manifestation of vitamin D

== VITAMIN D

The active form of Vitamin D is calcitriol (1, 25 di hydroxy cholecalciferol)

DAILY REQUIREMENT

The daily requirement of calcitriol is 200 to 400 IU

1 IU = 0.025 micrograms of cholecalciferol

DIETARY SOURCES

1. The cheapest source is sunlight
2. Fish liver oil is the richest source
3. Other sources are fish, egg yolk, margarine and lard

FUNCTIONS OF VITAMIN D.

1. Calcitriol increases the intestinal absorption of calcium and phosphorus by increasing the synthesis of calcium binding protein. This protein increases calcium absorption by the intestine.

2. In the osteoblasts of the bone, calcitriol stimulates calcium uptake for deposition as calcium phosphate. Thus calcitriol is essential for bone formation.

3. Calcitriol increases the reabsorption of calcium and phosphorus by the kidney and thus decreases their excretion in the urine.

DEFICIENCY OF VITAMIN D

There are 3 types of vitamin D deficiency:

1. Rickets
2. Osteomalacia
3. Renal osteodystrophy

RICKETS

1. Vitamin D deficiency in children is known as rickets.
2. In the absence of vitamin D the osteoblast proliferation is not accompanied by vascularization and mineralization at the normal rate.
3. The bones become soft.
4. Bending of long bones gives rise to deformities such as bow legs and knock knees.
5. The ankles, knees, wrists and elbows are swollen.
6. The fontanelles do not close properly giving rise to hot cross bun appearance of the head.
7. The ribs give a beaded appearance, known as ricket rosary.
8. The chest gives a pigeon breast appearance.
9. Teeth erupt late and are deformed

OSTEOMALACIA

1. Vitamin D deficiency in adults is known as osteomalacia
2. Osteomalacia is seen in pregnancy and lactation, when there is additional requirement of vitamin D and drainage of it in the milk
3. Osteomalacia is also seen in women who observe purdah and in areas where sunshine is scanty
4. In osteomalacia the bones become soft and are easily fractured
5. It particularly affects the pelvic bones

RENAL OSTEODYSTROPHY

1. It is also known as renal rickets
2. It is seen in patients with chronic renal failure

3. Renal rickets is mainly due to decreased synthesis of calcitriol by the kidney

4. It can be treated by the administration of calcitriol

Q 4. Functions and deficiency manifestation of vitamin C .

==VITAMIN C

Vitamin C is also known as ascorbic acid

FUNCTIONS

1. Vit C is required as a coenzyme in hydroxylation of proline and lysine

Hydroxyproline and hydroxylysine are important constituents of collagen

Thus vitamin C is required for collagen synthesis

2. Vit C is required for bone formation

3. Vit C enhances iron absorption by keeping it in the reduced ferrous

4. Vit C is essential for the hydroxylation of tryptophan to hydroxy tryptophan in the synthesis of serotonin

5. Vit C is required for the oxidation of P hydroxy phenyl pyruvate to homogentisic acid in tyrosine metabolism

6. Vit C is required for the reduction of dihydrofolate (FH_2) to tetrahydrofolate (FH_4).

Tetrahydrofolate (FH_4) is the active form of folic acid

7. Vit C is required for the synthesis of steroid hormones

8. Vit C is a strong antioxidant.

It spares vitamin A and vitamin E from oxidation

9. Vit C enhances the synthesis of immunoglobulins

10. Vit C increases the phagocytic activity of leucocytes

11. Vit C is required for the formation of mucopolysaccharides

12. Vit C is required for the functional activity of osteoblasts and fibroblasts

13. Vit C is required for the formation of ferritin

14. Vit C is required for the electron transport chain

15. Vit C activates the enzyme arginase and inhibits the enzymes urease and amylase

16. Vit C is required as a coenzyme for the conversion of dopamine to norepinephrine

17. Vit C is required for the formation of carnitine

18. Vit C is required for the alpha oxidation of fatty acids

19. Vit C plays a role in reduction of blood cholesterol level

20. Vit C plays an important role in the reaction of the body to stress

DEFICIENCY OF VITAMIN C

1. Vitamin C deficiency causes a disease called scurvy

2. The capillaries are fragile and there is a tendency to haemorrhage

3. The haemorrhage may be subcutaneous, subperiosteal or internal

4. Wound healing is deficient due to decreased formation of collagen

5. Poor teeth formation

6. Gums are swollen, spongy and bleed on slightest pressure

7. In severe infection there may be secondary infection, loosening and falling of teeth

8. Mineralization of the bone is poor and the bones are weak and easily fractured

9. Bones and joints are extremely painful

10 Hypochromic microcytic anemia

11.Elderly bachelors and widowers, who prepare their own food, are particularly prone to the development of vitamin C deficiency.This is called bachelor scurvy.

CHAPTER NINETEEN

MINERALS

Q 1. Functions of calcium

= **FUNCTIONS OF CALCIUM**

1. Calcium is required for bone formation
2. Calcium plays a role in muscle contraction

Calcium increases the interaction between actin and myosin

3. Calcium is necessary for transmission of nerve impulse
4. Calcium influences cell membrane structure
5. Calcium plays a role in the transport of water and ions across the cell membrane
6. Calcium activates the enzymes pancreatic lipase, ATPase and succinate dehydrogenase
7. Calmodulin is a calcium binding regulatory protein

Calcium calmodulin complex activates the enzymes adenylate cyclase and protein kinase

8. Certain hormones exert their action through the mediation of calcium and thus calcium acts as a second messenger or third messenger for such hormonal action e.g. – epinephrine and anti diuretic hormone
9. Calcium is required for the release of certain hormones from the endocrine glands e.g. insulin, parathyroid hormone and calcitonin

Q 2 .Factors affecting calcium absorption

== FACTORS AFFECTING CALCIUM ABSORPTION

FACTORS WHICH INCREASE CALCIUM ABSORPTION

1. Calcitriol (Vitamin D) induces the synthesis of calcium binding protein in the intestinal epithelial cells and increases calcium absorption

2. Parathyroid hormone increases calcium absorption by increasing the synthesis of calcitriol

3. Low pH (acidity) increases calcium absorption

4. Lactose increases calcium absorption

5. The amino acids lysine and arginine increase calcium absorption by increasing the solubility of calcium salts

6. Sugars increase calcium absorption.

Organic acids produced by the fermentation of sugars in the intestine increase the solubility of calcium salts and hence increase calcium absorption

FACTORS WHICH INHIBIT CALCIUM ABSORPTION

1. Phytates present in cereals form insoluble calcium salts and inhibit calcium absorption

2. Oxalates present in vegetables like cabbage and spinach form insoluble calcium salts and inhibit calcium absorption

3. High content of dietary phosphorus results in the formation of insoluble calcium phosphate and inhibits calcium absorption

4. Free fatty acids inhibit calcium absorption by reacting with calcium to form insoluble calcium soaps

This is particularly observed when fat absorption is impaired

5. High pH (alkaline conditions) inhibits calcium absorption

6. High content of dietary fibers interferes with calcium absorption

7. High content of magnesium in the diet decreases calcium absorption

8. High content of iron in the diet inhibits calcium absorption.

Q 3.Functions of iron

FUNCTIONS

1. Iron is a constituent of haemoglobin and myoglobin which are required for the transport of oxygen and carbon dioxide

2. Iron is a constituent of cytochromes which are required for the electron transport chain

3. Catalase is an iron requiring enzyme

Catalase destroys hydrogen peroxide

4. Peroxidase is an iron requiring enzyme

Peroxidase breaks down hydrogen peroxide and is also required for phagocytosis (killing of bacteria) by neutrophils

5. Iron requiring enzymes are

a) Xanthine oxidase

b) Cytochrome reductase

c) Acyl CoA dehydrogenase

Q 4 . Factors affecting iron absorption .

== **FACTORS AFFECTING IRON ABSORPTION**

FACTORS WHICH INCREASE IRON ABORPTION

1. Low pH (acidic pH) increases absorption

2. Vitamin C and glutathione increase iron absorption

3. Small peptides and amino acids increase iron absorption

4. In iron deficiency anaemia iron absorption is increased 10 times more than normal

5. Copper increases iron absorption

6. Meat, chicken and fish increase iron absorption

FACTORS WHICH DECREASE IRON ABSORPTION

1. Phytates present in corn, soya and cereals decrease iron absorption

2. Oxalates, present in leafy vegetables and chocolates decrease iron absorption

3. A diet with high phosphorus content decreases iron absorption

4. Tea, coffee and eggs decrease iron absorption

5. Dietary fibers decrease iron absorption

6. Alkaline pH decreases iron absorption

7. Impaired absorption of iron is found in malabsorption syndromes such as steatorrheoa

8. In patients with partial or total surgical removal of stomach / intestine, iron absorption is impaired

9. Parasitic infection (hookworm) decreases iron absorption

CHAPTER TWENTY

IMMUNOCHEMISTRY

Q 1.Structure and classification of immunoglobulins.

= **DEFINITION**

Immunoglobulins are a family of serum proteins, which function as antibodies

CLASSIFICATION

Immunoglobulins are classified into 5 types:

1. IgG
2. IgM
3. IgA
4. IgD
5. IgE

STRUCTURE OF IMMUNOGLOBULIN

1. The structure of immunoglobulin is known as the Edelman Gally model
2. Immunoglobulins are Y shaped
3. Each molecule has 2 heavy chains (H chains) and 2 light chains (L chains) – H_2L_2
4. The chains are held together by inter-chain disulphide bridges to form a bilaterally symmetric structure
5. Each chain is made up of a number of loops or domains of a constant size (100 amino acids)
6. The N terminal domain of each chain shows more variation and is known as the variable region or V region
7. The C terminal domain is relatively constant and is known as the constant region or C region

8. The zone where the variable and constant regions join is known as the switch region

9. The region of the H chain which is more susceptible to proteolytic attack and is more flexible, is known as the hinge region

10.The antibody binding site is known as the F_{ab} region

11. The complement fixing site is known as the F_c region

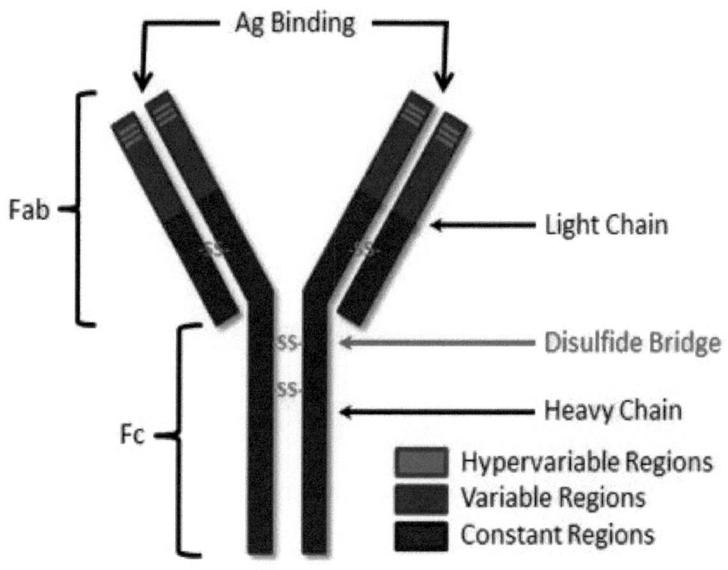

STRUCTURE OF IMMUNOGLOBULIN

Q2.Classify immunoglobulins and write one function of each class .

= **IMMUNOGLOBULINS**

DEFINITION

Immunoglobulins are a family of serum proteins, which function as antibodies

CLASSIFICATION

Immunoglobulins are classified into 5 types:

1. IgG
2. IgM
3. IgA
4. IgD
5. IgE

1. IgG

1. IgG comprises 70 to 80 % of the total immunoglobulins
2. Its serum level is 1200 mg %
3. It is a glycoprotein
4. The synthetic rate of IgG is 36 mg/kg/day

Function of IgG

IgG is the only immunoglobulin that can cross the placenta freely and is responsible for the protection of newborns during the first few months of life

On antigenic stimulation IgM is produced initially, followed later and ultimately replaced by IgG

IgM

1. IgM constitutes 7 % of the total immunoglobulins
2. Serum level of IgM is 100 mg %
3. It is a glycoprotein
4. IgM is a pentamer and has a J chain (joining chain)

Function of IgM

IgM it is the first antibody to appear in responce to initial exposure to an antigen.

IgA

1. IgA accounts for 10 to 20 % of the total immunoglobulins
2. The normal serum level of IgA is 200 mg %
3. It is a glycoprotein
4. IgA contains the J chain

Function of IgA

IgA provides the primary defence mechanism against local infections

IgA prevents access of foreign substances to the general immunologic system

IgD

1. IgD forms 0.2 % of the total immunoglobulins
2. Its serum concentration is 3 mg %
3. IgD is easily degraded by heat and proteolytic enzymes

Function of IgD .

1. IgD is the predominant immunoglobulin on the surface of B lymphocytes and may be involved in the differentiation of these cells
2. IgD has antibody activity towards

a) Penicillin
b) Milk proteins
c) Insulin
d) Diphtheria toxin
e) Thyroid antigen

IgE

1. IgE comprises 0.004 % of the total immunoglobulins
2. Its serum level is 10 to 70 micrograms %
3. IgE binds to certain specific antigens known as allergens

Function of IgE

IgE can fix to leucocytes and release mediators of inflammation on exposure to allergens

Thus IgE plays an important role in response of the individual in allergies.

Other Books By Author

1. Foundation Of Nursing 1 year Bsc Nursing: All Solved Questions and Answers.
2. NUTRITION AND BIOCHEMISTRY SOLVED QUESTIONS & ANSWERS : FIRST YEAR BASIC B.Sc. NURSING
3. MICROBIOLOGY : SOLVED QUESTIONS AND ANSWERS
4. COMMUNICATION AND EDUCATION TECHNOLOGY FOR NURSES BSc 2nd YEAR nursing: ALL SOLVED QUESTION AND ANSWERS (INCLUDING PREVIOUS YEAR)
5. Pathology and Genetics : Solved Question and Answers.
6. SOCIOLOGY: SOLVED QUESTIONS AND ANSWERS.

OTHER BOOKS COMING SOON STAY UPDATED

Contact Details

FOR FURTHER INFORMATION : PLEASE CONTACT ON BELOW INFORMATION

CALL ON 9130024431 .
EMAIL : rutwik61@gmail.com

THANK YOU .

BEST OF LUCK .

Book Availability

Book available On:

Book Availability on

OTHER BOOKS COMING SOON STAY UPDATED .....

9 798886 060188

Printed by Libri Plureos GmbH in Hamburg,
Germany